Christmas 2022 from Grandma Carol Hart

An Apple a Day

Also by Kent R. Hunter

Restoring Civility: Lessons from the Master

Who Broke My Church?
7 Proven Strategies for Renewal and Revival

Your Spiritual Gifts: Discover God's Plan for Your Life

The J-Dog Journey: Where Is Life?

Discover Your Windows: Lining Up with God's Vision

Your Church Has Personality:
Find Your Focus – Maximize Your Mission

The Jesus Enterprise: Engaging Culture to Reach the Unchurched

An Apple a Day

A Daily Dose for Everyday Faith

Kent R. Hunter
with Tracee J. Swank

Cover Design by PixelStudio, Fiverr.com/PixelStudio
Cover Copyright © Church Doctor Publishing
Formatted by Katie Erickson, Church Doctor Publishing

ISBN: 979-8-84-344105-0

Printed in the United States of America

"Everyone has a busy schedule these days. If you're like me, your life is lived around a calendar. Work, family, and church activities are just a few items that compete for my time. One thing—Bible reading—often is pushed down, rarely becoming a priority. Sound familiar? If so, you'll find *An Apple a Day* an exciting and helpful resource. In a few minutes' time, the authors introduce and illuminate a passage of Scripture and apply it to your life. It's worth your time to read each day. Take the time to read it today!"

—Gary L. McIntosh, speaker and author

"*An Apple a Day* is personal, practical, and powerful. You will want to begin every day with these inspiring insights from Scripture."

—Mitch Kruse, author of *Wisdom for the Road, Street Smarts from Proverbs,* and *Restoration Road*

"Daily doses of wisdom, with balance too! With people taking sides today, it's nice to discover this devotional guide by Kent Hunter and Tracee Swank. They give daily and practical prescriptions for spiritual growth and unity. Their daily doses of biblical wisdom will keep you grounded in God's Word. This devotional guide will sit on my nightstand!"

—Bob Whitesel, award-winning writer/scholar and directional leader of Leadership.church, MissionalCoaches.network & ChurchLeadership.university

"There is nothing more important than getting Christians into God's Word."

—David Maier, past Michigan District president of the Lutheran Church—Missouri Synod and founding member of Mission Partners Platform

Foreword

You might wonder: What in the world is a Church Doctor? Thanks for asking!

The Christian church is described many ways in the New Testament: the people of God, the citizens of the Kingdom, the sheep who belong to the Good Shepherd, and many more—including the body of Christ.

Every metaphor in Scripture describes the local church as a living organism. The church is alive! Churches are *birthed*. They can be *healthy*. They can get *sick*. Churches, sadly, can even *die*.

When your body faces challenges, if you're smart, you'll see a doctor. Doctors don't prescribe a one-size-fits-all remedy to every patient they see. That would be malpractice! Yet, many programs are sold, and used, as if every church was exactly the same, with the same challenges, at the same time.

Our team of Church Doctors are trained specialists in (1) *diagnosis*: what unique challenges your church is facing, right now; (2) *prognosis*: the prediction or forecast of the probable course or direction your church will take if those issues continue; and (3) *prescription*: a written direction for health, vitality, and growth, based on long-established, biblically authoritative help that provides health and growth to your unique body of Christ.

Your church, the body of Christ, is made up of cells, just like the human body. *You are one of those cells.*

Our team of Church Doctors is praying that this daily dose for everyday faith will greatly encourage you, and you will help your church be everything it can be for Jesus Christ, the Head of the body. Pray, with us, that everyone in your church would take a few minutes every day to be enriched by a daily dose for spiritual growth. God's Word is powerful!

There are 52 topics, one for each week of a year. Each week has seven "doses" of spiritual health from Scripture. Here's what we know: When you are spiritually healthy, you bring contagious vitality to your church. When churches get healthy, they become powerful communities that impact the world, one person at a time.

When people get healthy, they live longer. When they are spiritually healthy, they live forever. Yet, while they live on this earth, they live for others who don't know Jesus. As a contagious, healthy Christian, you will bring a holy infection to others, and God will change them for eternity. Pray with us for a Jesus epidemic. We pray it will begin with you, but not end there. God bless you! Enjoy the ride!

Introduction: About Apples

When I was a young boy, my grandmother said, "An apple a day keeps the doctor away." I'm guessing she was encouraging me to eat more fruit and less junk food!

There are some popular myths about apples as the concept appears in Scripture. For example, I've met some Christ-followers who say the tree of the knowledge of good and evil in the Garden of Eden must have been an apple tree. However, on close inspection of Genesis 2:8-9, it says:

"Then the Lord God planted a garden in Eden, in the East, and there He put the man He had formed. He made all kinds of beautiful trees grow there and produce good *fruit*. In the middle of the garden stood the tree that gives life and the tree that gives knowledge of what is good and what is bad (knowledge of everything)."

Verses 15-17 say, "Then the Lord God placed the man in the Garden of Eden to cultivate it and guard it. He told him, 'You may eat the *fruit* of any tree in the garden, except the tree that gives knowledge of what is good and what is bad. You must not eat the *fruit* of that tree; if you do, you will die....'" (Good News Translation, emphasis mine).

There is no mention of it being an apple tree. However, there is a prominent body part in the front of the throat, a little larger in males. It is commonly described as the Adam's apple. Actually, it got that name from the superstition that "it was caused by the forbidden apple sticking in Adam's throat," according to *Webster's New 20th Century Unabridged Dictionary*.

What is my point? As "Church Doctors," we have helped thousands of Christians on six continents grow in their spiritual health. Why? So they can reach more people for Jesus Christ. Our primary focus is on churches, but the "patients" we serve are people, just like you. They love the Lord and want to reach others for Jesus. They want their church to be more effective in mission and ministry. In our increasingly secular world, God's people can benefit greatly from a daily dose of biblical wisdom, applied to the challenges we face every day. The "Adam's apple" legend is just one example of drift from biblical wisdom.

God's Word does say that you are the apple of God's eye. This "apple" technically refers to the pupil in God's eye. The pupil is the most important part of an eye. The point? You are very precious to God. All people are important to the Lord. Every person—your non-Christian friends, relatives, neighbors, those at work or school—all are so valuable to God that Jesus died for them as well.

This one-year daily dose from God's one and only Book is not an in-depth Bible study. It shouldn't replace your small group or Bible class involvement. Yet, there is a very different approach in each *Apple a Day* reading. It does not approach you with Scripture to study and then apply it to your life. Instead, this "apple a day" begins with real-life challenges we all face. Your struggles are important to God, because you are the "apple of His eye"—very precious!

Each day ends with a Scripture verse that applies to the difficulties we all face. This approach makes the power of God's Word relevant, present, and profound in a personal way.

Each seven days begins a different area of life's issues. For each week, you focus on an issue from seven different angles. Life isn't simple. But God is never silent. He is always with us. Think about your family. Consider every person in your church. What might God do with a daily dose of everyday faith? This is what the Apple a Day Challenge is all about.

The Apple a Day Challenge is simple, but profound. Simply challenge and invite everyone in your church, those in your social network, those at work or school, to try one week using *An Apple a Day*. Ask them to pray about spending a short time in spiritual growth on a regular basis. Remind them that God's Word works for you, and it has had a profound impact on billions of people for centuries. With all the challenges of life, a daily dose from God could make all the difference. Invite others to give *An Apple a Day* a try. God will do the rest. He is never silent if we are listening!

What Is the Apple a Day Challenge?

The Bible says you are the "apple of His eye." It refers to the "pupil" of the eye, which is most precious. You are precious to God! That is the way God "sees" you. It is why He sent Jesus to die for you.

There is another kind of "pupil" in our language. A pupil is a student, someone who is learning, someone who is growing—sometimes called a disciple. 2 Peter 3:18 says, "…grow in the grace and knowledge of our Lord and Savior Jesus Christ."

The Apple a Day Challenge is a unique approach to spiritual growth. There are many great Bible studies available. Most start with a verse from Scripture. Some add a practical application portion at the end by providing content or questions for thought or discussion. *An Apple a Day* is organized opposite of that approach. It provides a daily reflection about the challenges of life. Like reverse engineering, this approach reverses Scripture application: (1) the challenge, (2) a "prescription" to learn God's approach, and (3) support from Scripture.

The *Apple a Day* approach is a user-friendly daily dose of inductive Bible teaching applied to the challenges of life. Each day includes a prescription for spiritual living. It is a daily spiritual vitamin that promotes mission health while strengthening your spiritual immune system.

Consider the well-known story of Jesus and the little children. Instead of teaching doctrine about how He loves little children, or beginning a sermon with "faith as a little child," the Scripture introduces us to a narrative, a real scenario: (1) Children come to Jesus. (2) The disciples see them as an interruption. (3) Jesus says, "Let the children come to me...." *Then,* Jesus gets to the "logical" point: (4) "...whoever does not receive the Kingdom of God like a child will never enter it" (Mark 10:15). We call it childlike faith—unconditional trust. This is an inductive, narrative approach.

In his introductory comments to Paul's letter to the Philippians, the translator of *The Message* version of Scripture, Eugene Peterson, writes:

> ...none of the qualities of the Christian life can be learned out of a book. Something more like an apprenticeship is required, being around someone who out of years of devoted discipline shows us, by his or her entire behavior, what it is. Moments of verbal instruction will certainly occur, but mostly an apprentice acquires skill by daily and intimate association with a "master," picking up subtle but absolutely essential things, such as timing and rhythm and "touch."
>
> ...Paul doesn't tell us that we can be happy, or how to be happy. He simply and unmistakably *is* happy. None of his circumstances contribute to his joy: he wrote from a jail cell,...
>
> ...circumstances are incidental compared to the life of Jesus, the Messiah, that Paul experiences from the inside.

This is why we formatted *An Apple a Day* the way we did. It starts with a challenge that most anybody can encounter. It is followed by a prescription from those who have been in the Christian faith for a long time—Church Doctors. At the end is a Scripture verse that, in most cases, actually uses some of the words in the content above. Beginning with a narrative and ending with a teaching together cause the Bible verse to "pop" with credibility and impact.

This is a totally different way of looking at applying Scripture to life. Yet, it appears to be the Bible's way. It is also the way good preachers start their sermons, with a real story about an issue of life and *then* moving toward the application of Scripture. The (1) inductive approach and the (2) use of story are powerful tools in the way Scripture points us to our Savior.

Each day is part of seven days focused on a common area of life—the theme for the week. At the end of each daily "dose" is the Scripture message that speaks to the unique challenge. The narrative of the challenge adds focus on the power of God's Word as a practical takeaway. The title, story, application, and Bible passage are unique for each daily reading, but the theme runs for a week. The content covers fifty-two weeks.

Many churches today are challenged to reach our increasingly secular society. *An Apple a Day* leverages narrative and applicable Scripture to support action and mission approaches. It focuses on encouragement to reach out to those who are unchurched in our social networks. The emphasis is not simply academic. Jesus is real. Faith in Christ works for everyday life.

The Apple a Day Challenge is to multiply impact—to be "fruitful and multiply." It reflects that disciples of Jesus make disciples of Jesus. It is not a program, but a movement. This approach invites you to encourage everyone in your church, small group, and social network to take the Apple a Day Challenge. It is also an ideal gift for friends, relatives, and those at work or school. It represents three to five minutes a day to focus on relevant issues, followed by an applicable Scripture. It is a small daily dose for everyday faith that takes three to five minutes to read. Never underestimate the power of God's Word and the dynamic of multiplication. Five minutes a day for 365 days equals 1,825 minutes, which is a little longer than 30 hours.

Invite everyone you know to join you in the one-year Apple a Day Challenge. Announce it in church. Email or text your friends. Post it on your website. Share it on social media. Put the solution to growing faith in the hands of everyone you know—give the book to family, friends, and coworkers. Move the movement. When you do, God gives you the power to change the nation and the world, one person at a time.

About the Use of Different Translations of Scripture

Most Christians have their "favorite" translation of the Bible. Sometimes there is confusion with our "favorite" and what we believe is the "best" translation. Actually, if "best" is your objective, you would want to learn Hebrew (for the Old Testament) and Greek (for the New Testament). Then you would have to choose the correct meaning intended by the authors God inspired to write the Scripture in the first place.

During four years of college, four years of seminary, and three years of graduate school, I (Kent) had to learn the basics of both Hebrew and Greek. After all that, I was nowhere near a scholar qualified to interpret the original texts into the English language. Some scholars spend their whole lives studying one book of the Old Testament or a letter or Gospel of the New Testament. They write commentaries that most pastors and teachers read to "unpack" the meaning.

Even more complicated is the fact that language continues to change in regard to relevant meaning. I grew up recognizing the words "thy" and "thou" in Scripture. But if I crawled into bed, kissed my wife goodnight, and said "I love thee," I might end up sleeping in the garage! Language carries meaning, and for meaning to stay the same, we must be willing to use different language! It's complicated!

After all my education, I studied for three additional years in the area of missions. Most pastors and Christian leaders who feel called to serve in a "foreign" mission field are required to be trained in "missiology." One of the many key insights of mission teaching is called "contextualization." If your heart language is English, but you want to reach people for Jesus who speak Spanish, the most effective approach is to speak Spanish to them. The best example of "contextualization" is Jesus: He showed up as a human baby—a Jew among the Jewish people.

In the research for *An Apple a Day*, we searched several Bible versions in the English language context, using the one that communicated with the most impact for the issues covered for each daily reading. The location of those verses is referenced. For further study, it is always a good idea to check several Bible versions. You can do it on your phone!

For the record, I have no favorite version of the Bible. For study purposes, I use several versions. However, if you were to press me on the subject and say, "Come on, Kent, which is your favorite?" I would respond, "The next one!" Our "prescription" as Church Doctors is this: When a new version comes out, read, study, and apply it. Then cross-reference it with other versions on your shelf. When you want to go deeper, refer to a commentary on that part of Scripture. We do it all the time.

Most of all, we pray you fall in love with God's Word. There is nothing like it. That is our prescription for the best material ever written—for life and for eternity!

Dedicated to Kingdom Encouragers

Jim and Marlys

Tom and Teri

Ben and Nancy

Mark and Gwen

Dan and Kathy

Jason and Laura

Jon and Esther

Janet

A crowd of prayer and support partners

An incredibly gifted staff and Board of Directors
at Church Doctor Ministries

Table of Contents

Theme: Change

Theme: Worship

Theme: Missions

Theme: Action

Theme: Self-Esteem

Theme: Witnessing

Theme: Financing

Theme: Personal Growth

Theme: Comfort

Theme: Influence

Theme: Spiritual Gifts

Theme: Worldview

Theme: Fellowship

Theme: Courage

Theme: Outreach

Theme: Involvement

Theme: Excellence

Theme: Generations

Theme: Integrity

Theme: Alive and Growing!

Theme: Friendliness

Theme: Decisions

Theme: Celebrate!

Theme: Relationships

Theme: People

Theme: Plan!

Theme: Posture

Theme: Risk

Theme: Conflict

Theme: Thanksgiving

Theme: Connection

Theme: Stewardship

Theme: Commitment

Theme: Joy

1 Sense of Urgency Theme: Time

In a hurry?

Heaven is! We need to get the good news about Jesus to the least, the last, and the lost—today! Can you sense the urgency? Sometimes, we're slow to take action because we're hung up on control. We like to wait for perfect conditions. But the world needs Jesus now. Patience is a fruit of the Spirit—not an excuse. Every day people die without Jesus.

Here's Our Prescription:

Commit yourself to action. Don't put off until tomorrow what you can do for God today. Serve your church—now. Become more active—now. Share what God has done in your life—now. Share your faith with your kids—now! Read your Bible—now. Rekindle your prayer life—now. After all, it's harvest time—now!

"If you wait for perfect conditions, you will never get anything done."
Ecclesiastes 11:4 (The Living Bible)

#2 The Ticking Clock Theme: Time

Got a second?

Thomas Edison said, "Everything comes to those who hustle while they wait." Did you know that during your life you'll spend six months sitting at traffic lights, a year searching for misplaced objects, and five years waiting in line? The clock is ticking!

Is it time you took time to consider how you spend time? Can you spend more time with God? More time for God? Time issues are never about quantity; we all get twenty-four hours a day. It's always about quality.

Here's Our Prescription:

Keep a time log for the next week. Where does your time go? Once you get a handle on where your time flies, you're set to improve. You'll even tell yourself: It's about time!

"Teach us to number our days and recognize how few they are; help us to spend them as we should."
Psalm 90:12 (The Living Bible)

#3 Time Bandits Theme: Time

Have you been robbed?

Time bandits—they're everywhere! Catching you unprepared, they steal precious time and give you nothing in return. They hide behind activities that are neither pressing nor important. Before you know it, the day is over, and you're not sure where it went.

Leisure activities balance your hectic life. However, how much is too much? Do you monitor how much time you spend watching TV, playing games on your phone, or surfing the Internet? Would making some changes increase your effectiveness? You have just one lifetime to impact your world.

Here's Our Prescription:

Continue working on your time log. Watch for time bandits that are stealing your life. Cut them out—while there's still time.

"...it is stupid to waste time on useless projects."
Proverbs 12:11 (Good News Translation)

#4 Use It or Lose It Theme: Time

Are you rich?

In this fast-paced world, money is not your most precious commodity—it's time! Time is a nonrenewable resource. It is super valuable! Have you ever worked on improving your time management? Managing time well isn't about getting things done. It's about getting the right things done! And, it's about getting the right things done right.

In the next thirty days, you'll make a thousand choices that affect your use of time. How will you make those decisions? Do your spiritual values influence your time management? You can't store time in a bank, your pocket, or a closet, so use it right, while you can!

Here's Our Prescription:

Let God manage more of your life. Then you'll know more about how to manage your time.

> *"...I run straight to the goal with purpose in every step."*
> *1 Corinthians 9:26a (The Living Bible)*

#5 Rest to Be Your Best Theme: Time

Are you balanced?

On the seventh day of creation, God rested. Rest doesn't ignore what is important. Rest has an important place all its own. Do you rack your brains trying to figure out how to add more activities to your life? Perhaps you should make a plan to rest, relax, reflect, refill, and recharge.

Life out of balance is unfulfilled, unhappy, and unfruitful. There's nothing lazy about resting. If you think there is, take that up with God. He set the example on the seventh day.

Here's Our Prescription:

Plan your days off in advance, create personal retreats, and protect your times of rest. Do it with conviction. Plan more time to be with God. Rest in Him, just like you focus on your career, family, or schoolwork. Rest to be your best!

"You have six days in which to do your work, but the seventh day is a day of rest dedicated to me."
Exodus 20:9-10a (Good News Translation)

#6 Burden of Busyness Theme: Time

"Can you help?"

Ever been asked to help at church or serve on a mission project? What's your response? Anyone can say, "I can't; I'm just too busy." We're all busy! Guess what? Serving God doesn't come from boredom. It comes from living out your spiritual priorities.

Your loaded calendar, your interruptive phone, emails, texts, your growing to-do list—do they bring you satisfaction? Do they supercharge you with fulfillment? There's nothing wrong with being busy. But, are you busy with the right things?

Here's Our Prescription:

Evaluate how busy you really are, then spend time reflecting on how God would adjust your priorities. Don't become too busy to realize you're too busy!

"...it is better to have only a little, with peace of mind, than be busy all the time...."
Ecclesiastes 4:6 (Good News Translation)

#7 Pull the Plug on Procrastination — Theme: Time

Proverbs says, "The lazy person is full of excuses, saying, 'If I go outside, I might meet a lion in the street and be killed!'" Sound ridiculous? Absurd? Do you ever make excuses? They likely sound just as stupid. Do excuses fuel your choice to "put off 'til tomorrow what you should do today"? Does that sound like you? Then it's time to pull the plug on procrastination.

Postponing your responsibilities makes life much harder. My friend John Maxwell said it well: "Pay on the front end, and play on the back end."

Here's Our Prescription:

Plan your work. Then, work your plan. If you're a chronic procrastinator, recruit an accountability partner to hold you responsible. Get help to get the job done—on time.

"Like a city whose walls are broken through is a person who lacks self-control."
Proverbs 25:28 (New International Version)

#8 The Seeds of Discouragement — Theme: Encouragement

Has life got you down?

A man found a barn where Satan keeps seeds to plant evil in people's hearts. Among those seeds were tiny seeds of discouragement. "Will they grow anywhere?" the man asked Satan. "Anywhere," said the devil, "except in the heart of a grateful person."

Being thankful is the antidote to discouragement. Problems, tensions, disagreements—they all lead to discouragement. So, ask God to guide you through those troubles with a *thankful* heart. It will expand your focus beyond the problems. It will fix your focus on God.

Here's Our Prescription:

Discouragement is a choice. Don't let the seeds of discouragement find a place in the soil of your heart. Ask God for an attitude of gratitude. Let God provide for your needs. Never give up on God. Why? God never gives up on you.

"...let us not get tired of doing what is right, for after a while we will reap a harvest of blessing if we don't get discouraged and give up."
Galatians 6:9 (The Living Bible)

#9 Encouragement Opportunities

Theme: Encouragement

Are you keeping an open eye?

C.S. Lewis said, "If Satan's arsenal of weapons was restricted to a single one, it would be discouragement." Are you discouraged? In your occupation, in your marriage, in your church, in your government? You need someone to come into your life to encourage you and give you hope. Pray for that person in your life. Hope is the fuel for encouragement.

What about you? Are you an encourager? Do you help people see the big picture? Can you show them the sun that always shines beyond the clouds? All you need is a compassionate heart and a loving spirit. Who, in your life, needs lifting? How can you encourage them?

Here's Our Prescription:

Become an encourager today. Watch those around you get fired up with hope. Watch their hope fuel your courage. Why? Courage eats discouragement for lunch.

"Let us think about each other and help each other to show love and do good deeds."
Hebrews 10:24 (New Century Version)

#10 The Journey

Theme: Encouragement

Are your bags packed?

Do you see your life as a journey? Or, are you focused only on destinations? Do you focus on success, happiness, and spiritual growth as realities limited only to your future? If you do, you are missing the excitement of your journey.

Here's Our Prescription:

Think of your life as a process. Every day, take another step in your Christian journey. Spiritual growth doesn't end when you finish school, become a church member, or retire. Celebrate the process your entire life. Each day is a step. Every step is an opportunity to learn and grow. You are a part in God's plan to fulfill His promises. Enjoy the process! With God, you are on a great journey!

"God has made us what we are, and in our union with Christ Jesus has created us for a life of good deeds, which he has already prepared for us to do."
Ephesians 2:10 (Good News Translation)

#11 Who's Your Soul Mate? Theme: Encouragement

Who knows you?

Your Christian life has its ups and downs. Discouragement can be overwhelming, especially when you're alone. That's why you should have a "soul mate"—a close, Christian friend to share joys, challenges, and spiritual struggles. Soul mates laugh, cry, rejoice, correct, pray, and encourage one another.

Sometimes soul mates have a lot in common. Occasionally, they are very different. Do you have a soul mate who has a commitment to Jesus and a loyalty to you? If so, you have a priceless gift. However, what if you don't have a soul mate?

Here's Our Prescription:

If you don't have a soul mate, pray. Ask God to lead you to someone. The right person will need you as much as you need your friend. Your soul mate will lift your spirits and motivate you to serve the Lord in love. You will do the same for your soul mate. Soul mates discover the win/win blessings of God.

"Two are better off than one, because together they can work more effectively. If one of them falls down, the other can help him up. But if someone is alone…there is no one to help him."
Ecclesiastes 4:9-10 (Good News Translation)

#12 Christian Coals

Theme: Encouragement

Are you hot for God?

Christians are a lot like coals in a barbecue. Separate them, and they lose their spiritual heat. Their spiritual fire goes out. Place them together, and they warm each other. A proven way to increase your heat for God's work is to get around other Christians who are already on fire.

One of the reasons God put you in a church is to warm your faith through the encouragement of others. You can be involved in a Bible study, fellowship group, or a team to provide a service to others.

Here's Our Prescription:

Spend more time with other Christians who want to set the world on fire for God! You'll catch fire. Like anyone else, you need to be connected. Together, we light up our world.

"For this reason we never become discouraged....our spiritual being is renewed day after day."
2 Corinthians 4:16 (Good News Translation)

#13 God's Encouragement Theme: Encouragement

Are you under attack?

A man once told me, "I've got so many troubles that if anything happens today, it'll be two weeks before I can even worry about it!" Some days are like that. It's frustrating when it seems everything goes wrong. It feels like you're under attack.

The Christian life isn't easy. Have you noticed? However, Jesus said, "…for he who is in you is greater than he who is in the world" (1 John 4:4, Revised Standard Version). In the battle of life, God wins. Today, you might feel like you're in a battle. However, you are never without weapons.

Here's Our Prescription:

Read, study, and pray over God's Word. Scripture is your weapon against discouragement. When David was discouraged, he let God encourage him. Let the Lord speak words of encouragement to you. You will experience victory. You have God's Word on it!

"I will praise the Lord no matter what happens. I will constantly speak of his glories and grace." – David Psalm 34:1 (The Living Bible)

#14 Be an Encourager

Theme: Encouragement

Do you need a lift?

In South Windsor, Connecticut, people were convinced the police had gone crazy. They were pulling over cars driven by people who were obeying the speed limit, using their turn signals, and wearing seatbelts. To everyone's surprise, the officers were giving drivers gift certificates as rewards! Would that encourage you to obey the traffic laws?

Most people have a tendency to become what you encourage them to be, not what you nag them to be. When I go through airport security, I tell each person, "Thank you for keeping us safe." They often say, "Thank you." Even when they don't, it helps *my* attitude!

Here's Our Prescription:

When you see someone working with diligence, tell them you appreciate it. Encourage those at church who give their best efforts. Be sincere. Be positive. Be a powerful influence in someone's life today. Write a note of thanks. Say a kind word. Share an uplifting thought. Be an encourager. Then watch what it does for *you*!

"We should help others do what is right and build them up in the Lord."
Romans 15:2 (New Living Translation)

#15 Hearsay Theme: Speech

Did you hear?

The bulletin read: "The pastor's message today is, 'Stop the Gossip,' after which the choir will sing, 'I Love to Tell the Story.'" It seems the things that go in one ear and out the other aren't as harmful as what goes in one ear, gets all mixed up, then slips out somebody's mouth! That is how gossip wrecks relationships.

Gossip doesn't have to be false or negative to be evil. There's a lot of truth that shouldn't be passed around. Why? It hurts people. You can be a powerful influence among your friends if they know you don't gossip. They'll know you're safe, reliable.

Here's Our Prescription:

Don't tear down anybody, ever. Build people up according to their needs. You will become a relational gift to others. Don't you think our world needs that?

"Do not use harmful words, but only helpful words,
the kind that build up and provide what is needed...."
Ephesians 4:29 (Good News Translation)

#16 Second Opinion Theme: Speech

Do you confront?

A man went to his physician for his yearly checkup. The doctor told him he had a terminal illness. Surprised, the man said, "Well, I want a second opinion!" The doctor shrugged his shoulders and replied, "OK, you're ugly, too."

Sometimes there's a fine line between honesty and love! Confronting others in a spirit of love is important if you want healthy relationships. God will help you to speak the truth in love if you ask Him. What about your motive? Is it to help them grow? Improve? Heal?

Here's Our Prescription:

Be honest, not rude. Be loving, not crude. Watch your tone, discipline your body language, and monitor your mood. You communicate more than you say with words. Be a champion for honesty. Speak in love to those who need direction. And watch your relationships soar!

"...have a sincere love for other believers, love one another earnestly with all your heart."
1 Peter 1:22 (Good News Translation)

#17 Make a Sandwich Theme: Speech

What's that recipe?

A psychologist was seeing a client for the very first time. He asked gently, "So, why don't you think people like you?" His patient sat up on the couch and said, "How should I know, you overpriced fathead?"

There are many ways you can correct, discipline, and instruct. Perhaps the best guidance comes from the Apostle Paul. He was the overseer of several new churches. They required a lot of correction. Yet, he always did it in love. He began by saying something positive about those he was addressing. Then he confronted them on the critical issues. Then, he ended with another round of positive comments.

Here's Our Prescription:

Try Paul's "sandwich method" of correction: praise/tough love/praise. It is the spiritual approach. And it works! Do you think that would improve our world? Let it start with you. Change your world, one person at a time.

> *"So then, we must always aim at those things that bring peace and that help strengthen one another."*
> *Romans 14:19 (Good News Translation)*

#18 Dirty Laundry Theme: Speech

Do you air dirty laundry?

At a local restaurant, a manager put up a sign as a reminder that the whole restaurant was NON-SMOKING. On Sunday mornings, the place was filled with churchgoers. By that afternoon, a busboy said, "They may not smoke, but you ought to hear them complain! If we had a NO-COMPLAINT section, it would be empty!"

Do you air the dirty laundry about your church in front of others? Do you show your frustrations in public? Who would ever attend your church if you rarely say anything positive about it? Problems don't get solved until they get faced.

Here's Our Prescription:

Don't air your church "dirty laundry" in public. Instead, deal with it in your church family. Work to diagnose the real issues, and learn what you can do to help fix them. In public, around unbelievers, always sit in the NO-COMPLAINT section. Let others know what is great about your church.

"May God who gives patience, steadiness and encouragement help you to live in complete harmony with each other – each with the attitude of Christ toward the other."
Romans 15:5 (The Living Bible)

#19 Correction! Theme: Speech

Do you have a problem?

Susan said something that offended Carol. So, what did Carol do? She told Sally and Mary about it! Though Carol was offended, she made the whole situation worse by blabbing it to others.

So, how would you deal with that situation, if Susan offended you?

Here's Our Prescription:

Read Jesus' amazing direction in Matthew 18. He said you should go directly to the person and confront her in love. If she doesn't listen to you, then go back again and take another person along as a witness. Don't involve anyone else. It's none of their business. If you resolve conflicts face-to-face, you will honor God, eliminate gossip, and create stronger unity among your friends. Become a Matthew 18 communicator. It's tough, but it's real love. Actually, it's tough love! And, oh yeah, it applies to emails, texting—every form of communication.

"'If a fellow believer hurts you, go and tell him – work it out between the two of you.'"
Matthew 18:15 (The Message)

#20 The Rudder — Theme: Speech

What did you say?

The Bible says the tongue is like the rudder of a ship. It's small, but it can steer the whole ship. You've got two ears, but only one tongue. Your Creator is sending you a message. The good news is that your tongue has a doubly reinforced fence—your teeth and your lips!

Go back and evaluate the last twenty-four hours. Has your tongue worked for good or for bad? Have you been part of the problem or part of the solution? Do you help or hurt in the lives of your friends, family, and church? Don't let the media or a late-night talk show host shape your approach. Look to your Creator.

Here's Our Prescription:

Ask God for the discipline to avoid saying anything that would divide, discourage, or destroy. Instead, use your tongue to share the life-giving, love-binding, uplifting, forgiving, restoring message of Jesus. Could your little tongue make a big difference—and benefit eternity? Yes!

"...we all make many mistakes. For if we could control our tongues, we would be perfect and could also control ourselves in every other way."
James 3:2 (New Living Translation)

#21 Tough Love — Theme: Speech

What do you do?

Jesus gave great insight about tough love. Here's a picture of Jesus' teaching in action. Mary showed up late again for work. It really caused problems for Elaine, who was working on a project with Mary. So, what did Elaine do?

As a Christian, she followed Jesus' teaching in Matthew chapter 18. She went directly to Mary. It wasn't easy. It never is. Here is what Elaine discovered. Mary has a sick child with a debilitating illness. Instead of hurting Mary through criticism or gossip, Elaine discovered an open door to help. Her choice to go directly to Mary made a difference. She made a friend. And Mary? She didn't gain a critic. She got a prayer partner.

Here's Our Prescription:

Do it by the book—God's book. Just think if everyone operated this way! Did you ever consider? You can change the world, one person at a time.

"...be kind to each other, tenderhearted, forgiving one another, just as God through Christ has forgiven you."
Ephesians 4:32 (New Living Translation)

#22 Who, Me? Theme: Leadership

Congratulations! You're a leader!

Now you may be saying, "Wait a minute! I'm no leader. I don't have a leadership role, and I don't know much about leadership!" Guess what? It doesn't matter! Because leadership isn't about holding a position; it's about influencing others.

You live your life in the context of relationships with others. You are always influencing someone: either positively or negatively. In what way do you influence—lead—others?

Here's Our Prescription:

Recognize this: Your words and actions *always* make an impact. Do you encourage everyone you meet? Do you try to find something positive in every challenge? Do you display a cheerful attitude? You may not always think of yourself as a leader, but you are. So, influence positively, and impact your family, those at work, your church, and community. Lead with love. Jesus did. You can, too, with His help.

"When others are happy, be happy with them. If they are sad, share their sorrow."
Romans 12:15 (The Living Bible)

#23 Asking for Help

Theme: Leadership

How do you ask?

Someone once said, "Never claim as a right what you can ask as a favor." Whether in your home, at work, or church, someday you're going to have to ask someone for help. *How* do you ask? Do you demand help? Do you place a guilt trip on others? Do you whine and complain until someone helps you, just to shut you up?

That's not how the Bible says you recruit help. Scripture says we should love one another. Love doesn't demand its own way.

Here's Our Prescription:

Start by helping others. If you want someone to help you, honestly share your need. Communicate your vision—why you need help. Share your excitement. Then give time to react. Ask your friend to pray about it. The way you ask is important. It's OK to ask for help. Jesus did. He asked twelve guys to help win the world. He asks you, too. You can ask for help. Just ask the right way.

"Love does not demand its own way."
1 Corinthians 13:5a (The Living Bible)

#24 Leadership Excellence Theme: Leadership

Are you leading the way?

I once had dinner with a man who had been the vice president of Intel. I was amazed at how dedicated that company is to excellence. Their aim is to have the best product presented the best way, delivered quickly. Unfortunately, some Christians don't have the same passion for excellence when it comes to sharing Jesus. It shows in the way they support their church, treat the staff, fail to serve, and hesitate to share their faith. As someone who influences others, you can lead the way—even the way to eternity!

Here's Our Prescription:

Commit to excellence on a personal level. Do the best you can to represent Christ to your friends. How? Learn all you can from Scripture. Grow all you can in your faith. You represent God's Son to the world. He's the best there is! Start today. Lead the way with excellence. God deserves your very best! What a great motto for Christians and churches and for you: the best "product"—salvation—presented the best way, delivered quickly.

"Good planning and hard work lead to prosperity, but hasty shortcuts lead to poverty."
Proverbs 21:5 (New Living Translation)

#25 Speaking of Support! Theme: Leadership

Are you supportive?

When terrorists attacked the United States, everyone was devastated. The president began to make plans. As he did, a whole nation—including those who didn't always agree with him—stood beside him. It created a powerful sense of unity. Do you see that among Christians? Do you support your Christian leaders unconditionally?

Here's Our Prescription:

Commit to a supportive attitude. You don't have to agree with every decision church leaders make. But you must support them when talking with others. If you hear others tear down your leaders, ask them to stop. As Christians, we are united in Jesus Christ—there is no place for slander. The biblical approach for unity begins with you and spreads to others. Vocalize your support, and be an example for others to follow!

"Appreciate your pastoral leaders who gave you the Word of God. Take a good look at the way they live, and let their faithfulness instruct you...."
Hebrews 13:7 (The Message)

#26 Leading by Living

Theme: Leadership

What would God say about your character?

Billy Graham once said, "When wealth is lost, nothing is lost; when health is lost, a little is lost; when character is lost, all is lost." As a Christian, your integrity is a witness to the world. When people see you living out your Christian values, they know you are for real. Then, they can believe God is for real. Your life can be the influence God intended it to be.

Every time you compromise your integrity, it makes it easier to do it again the next time. When you hold onto your integrity, it becomes easier to stand up for truth. When you fail, ask God for forgiveness—and strength for integrity.

Here's Our Prescription:

Remember that God is watching you. So are the people around you. Your life can be a powerful witness when you lead the way you live and live the way you lead. Your influence is contagious!

"The LORD detests people with crooked hearts, but he delights in those with integrity."
Proverbs 11:20 (New Living Translation)

#27 Servant Leadership — Theme: Leadership

Do you influence others?

Some people think leadership is all about getting others to do things for them. That's a poor view of how God sees leaders. In fact, the Bible says, if you want to influence others, serve and don't expect anything in return.

Most people go through life making deals. "If you do this for me, I'll do this for you." When you work, you get a paycheck. It is the world system: You help me; I'll help you. However, Jesus said that His Kingdom is not like this world (John 18:36).

Here's Our Prescription:

Give without the motivation of receiving. Love the unlovable. Look at how Jesus influenced others through servant leadership. You can only do that by letting go and letting God work through you. Servant leadership changes lives. Lives changed by Jesus change the world—one person at a time.

"Jesus...called the twelve disciples, and said to them, 'Whoever wants to be first must place himself last of all and be the servant of all.'"
Mark 9:35 (Good News Translation)

#28 Passing It On

Theme: Leadership

Are you a good ancestor?

You have incredible power to shape the next generation. It doesn't matter whether they are young people who know you from a distance, or they are your very own kids. Those who watch you are most likely to follow in your footsteps. It won't be based on what you teach, but on who you are. That is how you make a difference. It is the power of modeling.

Your family, your nation, and your world are only one generation away from heaven—or hell. You are planting powerful seeds in the next generation. What kind of seeds?

Here's Our Prescription:

Plant the seeds of your Christian faith. Let others see you live your faith every day. Don't put up a plastic front that hides life's challenges or your weaknesses. Real faith cries and struggles. Yet, real faith trusts God through good times and bad. Start today to be a good ancestor. Be real. Ask God to make you a powerful influence to the next generation.

"...you must do your utmost...and see that your faith carries with it real goodness of life."
2 Peter 1:5 (Phillips Translation)

#29 Whose Money Is That? Theme: Money

Is it yours?

Think for a moment about the money you earn. Picture it in your mind—think about holding it in your hands. Think about the amount you're paid. Now, in your mind, take it all away—and replace it with Jesus Christ. The Bible says it all belongs to Him. However, that's not the real issue. The issue behind the issue is this: Do *you* belong to Him?

Remember, everything you have, everything you are, belongs to God. When the church or another ministry asks for your help in partnership to do God's work, don't think of it as an obligation. Consider it a divine opportunity. Your resources represent the power of God to perform eternal miracles.

Here's Our Prescription:

Ministries need your financial help. God uses them to touch people for eternity. Make the most of your privilege to be a manager of God's resources. Choose wisely. Decide prayerfully. Give generously. Disperse carefully. Watch expectantly. In reality? It's all God's.

"Give freely and become more wealthy; be stingy and lose everything."
Proverbs 11:24 (New Living Translation)

#30 God Doesn't Want Your Money — Theme: Money

Not another one!

The congregation had just sung one of Fred's favorite songs. Fred was settling into his seat as Pastor Bob began his sermon. Suddenly, red flags went up in Fred's head. A wall rolled across his heart and a padlock clasped around his wallet. It was another sermon about giving money!

If you've got a hard heart about Christian finances, it's time to ask God to soften it: In truth, God doesn't want your money. He wants you! When He gets you, He gets everything—including your money. And why not? It's an important part of your life. Do you believe what God wants is best for you?

Here's Our Prescription:

Give your financial worldview to God. Open your ears. Open your heart. Let God's generosity in Christ touch your life—and your finances. How do you know God rules your life? One way is when you find yourself gladly opening your wallet—with joy.

"Honor the LORD with your wealth and with the best part of everything you produce. Then he will fill your barns with grain, and your vats will overflow with good wine."
Proverbs 3:9-10 (New Living Translation)

#31 Equal Sacrifice Theme: Money

Are you waiting for the right time?

When I was in seminary, I raised money for an outreach ministry. I asked the president of a huge company for a donation. He asked me if I gave ten percent back to God. I said I was just a poor seminary student. He said, "Do you think it's any more of a sacrifice when you're wealthy?" God is not interested in equal giving. His focus is on equal sacrifice.

Here's Our Prescription:

The Bible says to give as the Lord has given to you. If He gives you more, give more back to Him. If He gives you less, give Him back less. But keep the percentage the same. Forget about what you can afford. Focus on what you can give. Be a good manager of money. And remember: you can't outgive God.

"...Jesus said, 'Truly I tell you, this poor widow has put more into the treasury than all the others. They all gave out of their wealth; but she, out of her poverty, put in everything – all she had to live on.'"
Mark 12:43-44 (New International Version)

#32 The Joy of Generosity Theme: Money

Are you living generously?

Someone said, "The only way to really win with money is to hold it loosely—and be generous with it to accomplish things of value." I hope you have a positive attitude about generosity. If you do, then you know the true joy of giving.

It's not a law, but you get the impression from the Bible that it's a great idea to give generously to God's work through your local church. Many interpret the Scripture to say that ten percent is a minimum. There are ministries beyond your church, too. An additional five percent of your income can go a long way to help them.

Here's Our Prescription:

Would you like to experience a miracle? Give generously. Discover you can't outgive God. No one can explain it. You can only experience it. God blesses generosity. Here's the bottom line: Give because you love the Lord. Watch the impact it makes. Discover the generosity of God.

> *"Bring your full tithe to the Temple treasury so there will be ample provisions in my Temple. Test me in this and see if I don't open up heaven itself to you and pour out blessings beyond your wildest dreams."*
> *Malachi 3:10 (The Message)*

#33 Count Your Blessings Theme: Money

Do you have two hands?

Joe's a tough guy who often says, "Everything I have, I've gotten with these two hands." So I asked him, "Who gave you those hands?" Here's the challenge: If you don't recognize what God has given you, chances are you won't think much about giving back. And that hurts everybody, including you!

Here's Our Prescription:

Set aside time to write down all your blessings. (You might want to do this exercise with your family.) List the top ten or twenty blessings, but don't stop there. Thank God for each blessing. Then ask yourself, "What am I giving back?" Develop a strategy to give back to the God who gives you everything. If you have been blessed, be a blessing to others.

"...my God will meet all your needs according to the riches of his glory in Christ Jesus."
Philippians 4:19 (New International Version)

#34 Giving the Best — Theme: Money

What do you give?

I once heard an inner-city preacher say, "Don't give me your secondhand, worn-out clothes to give to the poor. If you really want to generate the power of hope, go out and buy new clothes for these people." That preacher really made me think! What about you? Do you give financial "leftovers" to God?

The Bible says to give to God's work off the top. The Scripture calls it "firstfruits" giving. It means He deserves the best. When we give our best, His work thrives.

Here's Our Prescription:

When planning your budget, don't end it with giving to God. Start it with God. Put His work first, not last. Take inventory of your giving. If you value God's love, would you give Him the best, or would you throw Him the leftovers? You know the answer. So, do it! Give God the best!

"While Jesus was in Bethany in the home of Simon the Leper, a woman came to him with an alabaster jar of very expensive perfume, which she poured on his head as he was reclining at the table."
Matthew 26:6-7 (New International Version)

#35 The God of Abundance — Theme: Money

What's your view?

Ever hear this? "I think with the population explosion, we're going to run out of food." Or, "Our budget is already stretched. We can't afford that." What about this approach? "As the population expands, God provides new insights and technology." Or, "The budget is maxed, but God will provide." How do you understand God? Is He a God of scarcity or abundance? Someone said, "If it's God's will, it's God's bill. God pays for what He orders."

Ever feel challenged about giving to God's work?

Here's Our Prescription:

Tape these words to your bathroom mirror, the dashboard of your car, your checkbook, or your computer—"You can't outgive God." Test Him, and He'll provide blessings. God promises to supply all of your needs. Your financial giving isn't an economic issue. It's a spiritual issue. Believe it!

"...every man is a fool who gets rich on earth but not in heaven."
Luke 12:21 (The Living Bible)

#36 God's Direction for You — Theme: Change

Do you resist change?

Ever feel like shouting, "Stop the world—I want to get off"? We live in a rapidly changing world. It's enough to stress you out—even as a Christian! Obviously, not all change is good. But like it or not, the concept of change is very biblical. After all, Jesus came to earth. That is a huge change! And He did it for us.

God wants to change you. He wants you to grow. He wants you to become an effective witness—a good representative for Him. Sometimes that includes change.

Here's Our Prescription:

When you are faced with change, determine your reaction: by whether or not it is what *God wants*. If it's God's plan for you, take a deep breath and allow it. If it isn't, resist it. Pray for God's direction. Look to Scripture for guidance. Ask a trusted friend for input. Demonstrate faith, trust, and openness. It will help you face all the change. You will not just be informed, but transformed.

> *"Do not conform yourselves to the standards of this world, but let God transform you inwardly by a complete change of your mind."*
> *Romans 12:2a (Good News Translation)*

#37 Growing Pains Theme: Change

Do you really want to grow?

Linda finally found a church with powerful preaching and teaching. What she was hearing was biblical, but soon she found herself feeling uncomfortable. Why? It was stretching her! Biblical truth helps you grow. Growth means change. And that is uncomfortable. Mark Twain said, "The only person who likes change is a baby with a wet diaper." Sometimes we don't change until we are uncomfortable!

Here's Our Prescription:

God is more interested in your character than in your comfort. He is more committed to your eternal growth than to your earthly satisfaction. Embrace the growing pains, and ask God to help you through them. He will give you the power to endure. In the process, you will learn that He can be trusted. If all Christians would let God grow them, you would see two results: more discomfort and a lot more spiritual fulfillment.

"Do not merely listen to the word, and so deceive yourselves. Do what it says."
James 1:22 (New International Version)

#38 Can't Change? Theme: Change

Have you ever said, "I can't change"?

While brushing my teeth, I realized my wife bought a different brand of toothpaste. I complained. She asked, "Did you try it?" I said, "Not yet." She said, "I hope you like it. It was on sale, and I bought *ten* tubes!" By the end of the second tube, I didn't notice the difference. By the third, I couldn't remember the name of the old brand!

Do you ever feel like you just can't change? God created a world in motion, which means everything is constantly changing. As maturing Christians, our lives change a lot!

Here's Our Prescription:

Before you get bent out of shape, say a little prayer, and take a little step forward. After a few steps, you'll probably say, "That wasn't so bad!" Can the "can't." Trust in God. You can change more than you think. And if you won't—you don't!

"Commit everything you do to the Lord. Trust him to help you do it and he will."
Psalm 37:5 (The Living Bible)

#39 Grumble, Grumble Theme: Change

Are you adapting well?

John F. Kennedy said, "Change is the law of life. And those who look only to the past or the present are certain to miss the future." Among Christians, most changes are initiated by those who mean well. They are trying hard to be faithful in a changing world. Whether they are right or wrong, how is your grumbling going to help?

Here's Our Prescription:

Don't grumble about changes at your church. Listen to those who can help you understand. Don't become part of the problem. Be a part of the solution. Your grumbling doesn't help your attitude, and it surely doesn't inspire others. Get behind your leaders. Cheer them on and encourage them. Would your church thrive with a positive atmosphere? Absolutely it would! Would your family? Would you?

"The prudent understand where they are going, but fools deceive themselves.
Proverbs 14:8 (New Living Translation)

#40 Correct Change Theme: Change

Are you prepared for change?

Being a Christian has many challenges. We live in a changing world. Most unchurched people don't get excited about what Christians believe. Sadly, all too often, we have blown our credibility. Therefore, we have to prove our relevance—demonstrate that God is real.

Often, that requires change. We need to be attractive. We must speak the language of those outside the faith. We won't change the truth of the Bible. Jesus is always the same. But methods and programs must change. So, what will you do? Will you say, "We've always done it that way"? Or, will you change, for the cause of Jesus Christ?

Here's Our Prescription:

Be careful about saying, "But we've always done it that way." Make the choices that will make the changes that will reach others for eternity.

"Intelligent people are always ready to learn. Their ears are open for knowledge."
Proverbs 18:15 (New Living Translation)

#41 Agent or Roadblock? Theme: Change

How do you respond?

Winston Churchill said, "There is nothing wrong with change, if it is in the right direction." Some changes are beneficial; others become obvious mistakes. Appropriate change is what allows the Christian faith to remain relevant in a changing world. How do you respond to appropriate change? The Christian message must never change. The delivery systems must always change.

Are you a change agent or a roadblock to the mission of Jesus? If you are unwilling to change, it means you are unable to grow. To grow is to change.

Here's Our Prescription:

Spend some time thinking about how you deal with change. What would you die for? Write down everything in your spiritual life that doesn't really matter. Don't major in the minors. Jesus never changes. But, our constantly changing world needs Jesus—now!

"Jesus Christ is the same yesterday, today, and forever."
Hebrews 13:8 (New King James Version)

#42 Progress and Change Theme: Change

Are you ready for change?

A man once told me: "I'm one hundred percent for progress. It's all this change I'm against." In our homes, at work, even at church, we tend to find our comfort zones. When people make changes that disrupt—the war is on! For that reason, many people hate change. Yet, good change brings progress.

What is more important: your comfort or the impact of your faith? Are you more interested in what *you* want or what *God* wants? Do you see Christianity just for yourself or also for others? Do you submit to those who lead, or are you rebellious?

Here's Our Prescription:

Step back and look at change from the eternal perspective. Is God in it? If so, shouldn't you be, too?

"...may your will be done on earth as it is in heaven."
Matthew 6:10b (Good News Translation)

#43 24/7 Worship Theme: Worship

Do you ever stop?

Is worship something you just do at church? Or, is it a lifestyle you live 24/7? If I woke you up at three in the morning, would you have a worship thought? Technically, worship is giving praise and honor to God. It reflects how important God is in your life. Ever think about it? You can have a "God thought" anywhere, anytime—not just at church! Any focus on God is an act of worship. That doesn't make you a "fanatic," just God's "fan."

Here's Our Prescription:

Place worship reminders around your life. Put praying hands on your desk at work or a Christian bookmark in a book. Wear a cross on a chain around your neck. There are countless spiritual reminders. They can help you "worship without ceasing." Worship is not just a church event. It is a living lifestyle of praising God. In fact, as you read this, you are in an act of worship. You are demonstrating that you value God.

"O come, let us worship and bow down, let us kneel before the Lord, our Maker!"
Psalm 95:6 (Revised Standard Version)

#44 MIA — Theme: Worship

Are you missing worship?

It happens to almost every Christian at one time or another. A disruption of life occurs, and you slip away from regular worship. Before you know it, you are out of the routine. At first, you may not miss worship, but God misses you. And so do your fellow believers. You may be slowly drifting from spiritual engagement. You are MIA—missing in action—God's action.

Here's Our Prescription:

Ask yourself, honestly, don't you feel better after you worship God? Think about this: What keeps you away? How will you change that? Make a plan right now. Do you need to try a worship time that better fits your lifestyle? Maybe you need to reprioritize your life. Perhaps you would respond to a different style of worship. Or, you may need to find another church. Whatever it is, do it for God, do it for you, and do it soon!

"Let's keep a firm grip on the promises that keep us going.... Let's see how inventive we can be in encouraging love and helping out, not avoiding worshiping together...."
Hebrews 10:23-25 (The Message)

#45 POW

Theme: Worship

Do you have a worship life?

When life is important, most people block out time. You do it for the dentist. You do it for your favorite television shows. You do it to check your email. You do it to read the paper or check your phone. Do you do it for your spiritual growth? If not, maybe you need what I call POW—personal opportunities to worship. They are everywhere!

Here's Our Prescription:

Deliberately block out time—to spend time—with God. Set aside personal worship time every day. Make it a "holy habit." You can pray, silently, in an elevator. You can worship in your car. You can listen to Christian music. You can read the Bible on your lunch hour. Put everyday worship in your life. You will begin to live a life of worship—a powerful one! POW! There are personal opportunities to worship everywhere! (You just experienced one!)

"...we worship God by means of his spirit and rejoice in our life in union with Christ Jesus."
Philippians 3:3 (Good News Translation)

#46 Heart Language Theme: Worship

Do you like what you hear?

Terry and Sally attended the early service. It was the traditional worship hour, and it had hymns they knew. However, their teenagers didn't respond well to the style of music or the formality. So, they decided to put their personal preference aside and attend the contemporary service. It was the same biblical message—in a different "package."

Every generation, every culture, has its own "heart language." It includes styles, instruments, tempos, and volume. It is all part of God's amazing imagination. God has a unique heart language for each person, every generation.

Here's Our Prescription:

God's truth impacts you more when it is packaged in your heart language. If you have children, here is the biblical principle: The more mature Christian always subordinates his or her worship preference to that of the less mature believer. The model? Jesus came down to earth!

"In the past God spoke to our ancestors through the prophets many times and in many different ways. But now in these last days God has spoken to us through his Son."
Hebrews 1:1-2a (New Century Version)

#47 Spirit and Truth Theme: Worship

Got it together?

Bob and Mary were describing their respective churches. Bob said, "The preacher at my church delivers good messages, but the music and worship are boring." Mary said, "My church has uplifting music, but the preacher talks politics and current events." Bob and Mary are missing different, but important, elements of worship.

The Bible says, "Worship in spirit and in truth." Worship should make sense to you *and* touch your own "heart language." Heart language reflects the words of your dreams. It includes the music you listen to in your car. The truth element has only one source: Scripture. God is not interested in opinions. He speaks from the Bible. Why? It's *His* Word. That is *truth*. Music and preaching are the delivery systems.

Here's Our Prescription:

Analyze your worship experience. Is it spirit and truth? When you have both, God's Kingdom grows in you and through you, to others.

> *"Those who live as their human nature tells them to, have their minds controlled by what human nature wants. Those who live as the Spirit tells them to, have their minds controlled by what the Spirit wants."*
> *Romans 8:5 (Good News Translation)*

#48 A Joyful Noise Theme: Worship

Is your church's worship changing?

The Bible says, "Make a joyful noise to the Lord." Worship and music are important elements of the Christian life. However, the way we make a "joyful noise" is always changing. In 1977, the number of pipe organs sold to churches was 222,000. By 2005, it dropped below 20,000 per year. Now, it's very few.

Here's Our Prescription:

Come to grips with two realities: (1) Change is hard; and (2) Christian worship is always changing. The style, methods, dress code, and language change to meet the culture of every age. If they don't, the impact fades. When the style fits the culture of the people you're trying to reach: (1) It touches their "heart language"; and (2) it has greater impact. The truth *always* stays the same. Yet, God creates new ways to reach people in the context of their cultures. It all demonstrates that there is more than one way to "make a joyful noise to the Lord." Keep the truth. Don't worship the style.

"I kept my bearings in Christ – but I entered their world and tried to experience things from their point of view. I've become just about every sort of servant there is in my attempts to lead those I meet into a God-saved life."
1 Corinthians 9:21-22 (The Message)

#49 Excited Eyes Theme: Worship

Are you looking for the best?

After the church service, Mary complained to her husband, Fred, "Did you hear how often Pastor John repeated himself?" Fred replied, "No." "Well, did you notice the ushers missed three rows during the offering?" Fred replied, "No." "Did you hear that screaming kid?" "No." Mary sighed, "Honestly, Fred, I don't know why you bother going to church!" What is your focus in worship?

Here's Our Prescription:

Worship with *excited eyes*—looking for what God is doing. Enter with a *hungry heart*, ready to encounter your living Lord. Step in with a *miracle mindset*, eager for a God encounter. Develop an *attitude of gratitude* for the privilege to worship the Creator of the universe. Breathe in *eager anticipation*. You are about to experience the living Lord.

> *"Your worship must engage your spirit in the pursuit of truth. That's the kind of people the Father is out looking for: those who are simply and honestly themselves before him in their worship. God is sheer being itself– Spirit. Those who worship him must do it out of their very being, their spirits, their true selves, in adoration."*
> *John 4:23b-24 (The Message)*

#50 Need a Challenge? Theme: Missions

Are you ready for a shot of spiritual adrenaline?

I spend most of my time consulting, writing, and speaking at conferences. Once in a while, I get to take a group on a short mission trip to another country. It is good to take the plunge, experience risk, stretch spiritual muscles, and step out of your comfort zone. A mission trip is a great opportunity for the Holy Spirit to work in your life. Sound like an intriguing challenge?

When you are separated from your cell phone, shower, bed, and email—immersed in another culture—your life is forever changed. I can't explain it. It's a God thing!

Here's Our Prescription:

If you have never been on a short-term mission trip, don't delay any longer! It can be in another country or a different culture in your own nation. Take the risk. Learn to trust God at a whole new level. Experience how you impact others. Shine your light. Discover how God impacts you!

"You are the light of the world."
Matthew 5:14a (Revised Standard Version)

#51 Lens Checkup Theme: Missions

What do you see?

Author Darrow Miller says, "We all wear a set of lenses, but are unaware that they exist." What is he talking about? He's talking about your worldview—the way you see the world and understand how it works. It determines how you think, act, and live your life. Some people have a worldview that focuses entirely on themselves. That is a puny, "me-centered" world. It is not healthy. Do you need a "lens" correction?

Here's Our Prescription:

Sign up to be a short-term missionary. Feel how others from a different culture live. Visit an impoverished area of the world. Watch them "light up" when you show up. Discover their attitude of gratitude, because you care. It will forever change how you see and understand your world. God will change your worldview and help you change the world.

"You are the salt of the earth; but if salt has lost its taste, how shall its saltiness be restored?"
Matthew 5:13a (Revised Standard Version)

#52 Point of No Return Theme: Missions

Do you give beyond?

Curt and his mission team spent two weeks in Nigeria. During that trip, they gave basic medical care to the poor, provided bandages and hygiene products, distributed Bibles, and provided Christian messages with puppet shows for children. By the end of the trip, they were exhausted and exhilarated, bubbling with "enthusiasm."

The word "enthusiasm" comes from Greek. It literally means "in God." Engaged in God's work, you will experience divine enthusiasm and spiritual excitement.

Here's Our Prescription:

Take a mission trip to a different culture. You will *catch* what can't be *taught*: the thrill of giving without receiving. The more you give, the more others see God's love through you. You won't get paid. You come home with riches money can't buy and spiritual fulfillment that lasts for eternity.

"You'll not likely go wrong here if you keep remembering that our Master said, 'You're far happier giving than getting.'"
Acts 20:35b (The Message)

#53 Capture the Experience

Theme: Missions

Are you ready for a spiritual adventure?

I watched as the missionary showed her pictures of very different people. They were poor, but smiling. Struggling, yet happy. The crowd listened to the sense of adventure she felt spreading God's Word in southeastern India. It was nice, but it is her story. Yet, it could be yours.

Here's Our Prescription:

Experience a mission trip for yourself. Watching a slide show is not like being there. You can observe the scenery through pictures. You can even be moved by God's love for people. But you *become* God's transforming work when *you* are there. When you touch it, smell it, feel it, hear it, experience it; when you eat the food and sleep on a different kind of bed—you are transformed forever. When you return, you will be *mission contagious.* You will plant seeds for others. You will multiply others who catch it from you.

> *"Jesus said to his followers, 'There are many people to harvest but only a few workers to help harvest them.'"*
> *Matthew 9:37 (New Century Version)*

#54 Open for God's Business? Theme: Missions

Are you open to God?

Henri Nouwen said, "Prayer is listening to God. It's openness. God is always speaking; he's always doing something." How open are you to God? My friend needed a challenge. So, I asked him to come along on a ministry trip to the Amazon jungle. However, he immediately refused. Maybe he wasn't open to what God wanted to do in his life. Perhaps the timing wasn't right.

What is a "mission trip," really? It is an opportunity for God to move you out of everyday life. When you are on unfamiliar soil, you experience utter dependence upon Him. When everything is different, you encounter two dimensions at a deeper level: your humanity and God.

Here's Our Prescription:

Spend time in prayer. Ask God where He wants you to join Him. That is a wonderful and dangerous prayer! It may take you places you've never been, not just geographically, but spiritually. You will never be the same. And, you will probably want to do it again! Further, everyone around you will catch it! You will be different—forever.

"And when the Holy Spirit comes on you, you will be able to be my witnesses in Jerusalem, all over Judea and Samaria, even to the ends of the world."
Acts 1:8 (The Message)

#55 A Bigger World(view) Theme: Missions

What do you see?

Have you ever seen water go down the drain the other way? It does in the southern hemisphere. Ever looked at the sky and seen different stars? You can't see the Big Dipper in South Africa. But the Southern Cross is there! Traveling to another land stretches your worldview. It is natural to think the world revolves around you, your community, your country. Yet, it doesn't. Why is that important? Because the way you see your world impacts how you understand the greatness of God. You will become a *world Christian.*

Here's Our Prescription:

Get out of your community, your country, even your hemisphere. Experience reality that stretches your worldview. It will expand your vision. You will experience God in a new way. In the process, you will become a "big-picture" thinker. You will grow spiritually—to a whole new level. Take the mission plunge!

"...grow in the grace and knowledge of our Lord and Savior Jesus Christ."
2 Peter 3:18 (Good News Translation)

#56 Planning Your R&R Theme: Missions

Do you need a different kind of vacation?

Have you been working hard? Need a break? Looking for refreshment? You need some R&R. For most, that means "rest and relaxation." That is great and necessary, once in a while. But this R&R represents Reach out and Revolutionize.

Here's Our Prescription:

Take a short-term "mission trip," even if it is to a different cultural area nearby. By serving others less fortunate, you discover the refreshment of giving rather than receiving. Stepping foot on different soil offers fulfillment you can't get at a resort or the excitement you expect from an amusement park. You will feel warmth you won't get at the beach. You will reach spiritual heights that you won't experience climbing mountains. You will return with a different kind of R&R: not rest and relaxation, but recharged and refreshed. Guaranteed!

> *"...I keep praying that this faith we hold in common keeps showing up in the good things we do, and that people recognize Christ in all of it. Friend, you have no idea how good your love makes me feel, doubly so when I see your hospitality to fellow believers."*
> *Philemon 1:6-7 (The Message)*

#57 In the Game Theme: Action

Are you in the game?

A man spoke to the pastor about becoming a church member. He began, "I really don't want to do anything or give anything, and I'll show up when I feel like it." The pastor said, "Sorry, but you're at the wrong place. Here is the address." The man went to the address and found himself standing at the entrance to a cemetery.

Being a Christian means getting in the "spiritual game." Are you a player or a spectator?

Here's Our Prescription:

Look at the Great Commission given to every Christian: "Go make disciples…" (Matthew 28:19-20). It doesn't say, "You all come," or "Sit in church and spiritually vegetate." Ask God how He wants you to get involved. Take a little step into the mission. A Dutch proverb says, "He who is already outside his door has the hard part of the journey behind him." Sometimes, that first step is all you need. Christianity is a movement. So, move. Get in the game, and others will join you. As a believer, you are on a mission. Let go, and let God use you to change the eternal destiny of others. You will never go back to the bleachers, and a heavenly crowd will cheer!

"…I tell you, there is joy before the angels of God over one sinner who repents."
Luke 15:10 (Revised Standard Version)

#58 Movin' Out Theme: Action

Are you stuck inside?

Harry is involved in several activities at his church. He sings on the worship team and helps with building maintenance. But nothing fires up Harry like serving at the local soup kitchen. He says, "Sometimes it's good to get outside the walls of our church!"

Jesus said, "Love your neighbor as yourself." Often, that means getting out of your comfort zone and onto the mission field.

Here's Our Prescription:

Find a ministry that impacts your community. Help turn your church inside out. Jesus didn't just say, "Y'all come." His mission challenge is to "Go!" You could help the poor, visit prisoners, or lead a Bible study at the coffee shop. You could start a gathering where unchurched or new Christians can learn more about God. You can meet at a restaurant, a park, or in your home. Unchurched people are often more comfortable meeting away from the church building. You are on a mission from God. Move out!

"Go out into the world uncorrupted, a breath of fresh air in this squalid and polluted society. Provide people with a glimpse of good living and of the living God. Carry the light-giving Message into the night…."
Philippians 2:15 (The Message)

#59 Guts and Ruts Theme: Action

Ever feel like you are in a rut?

Zig Ziglar says, "If you wait until all the stoplights are green, you'll never leave the driveway!" Have you ever delayed acting because of potential challenges? Dangers? Potholes of life? Are you unsure of yourself, or not sure if it's the right time? Are you concerned you might not have the energy, intelligence, skills, or discipline?

Or, are you procrastinating? The Bible says in Ecclesiastes, "If you wait for perfect conditions, you'll never get anything done!" Moving out in faith requires taking risks. The fewer risks you take, the deeper your rut becomes. Christians have these challenges, and so do churches—even denominations!

Here's Our Prescription:

When was the last time you *risked* for God? Perhaps it was sharing your faith with a stranger or accepting a ministry assignment. It takes guts to leave ruts. Start praying—and living by faith. God's light is green. Leave your spiritual driveway.

"Whatever I have, wherever I am, I can make it through anything in the One who makes me who I am."
Philippians 4:13 (The Message)

#60 Service with a Smile Theme: Action

Are you a good example?

Tom is a young man growing in his faith. One day he helped deliver Christmas presents to inner-city families. His friend Dan saw the joy and joined him. In two weeks, three more came along. Tom never "recruited" anyone. He became a magnet of enthusiasm. He didn't build a program. He never put up posters, never begged for helpers. Tom started a movement. Tom didn't beg for volunteers. He attracted followers.

Here's Our Prescription:

Christianity is a movement. If you get the calling and go to work, you move the movement. Most people want to get involved in worthy causes. Get excited about serving God. Discover your gift area and calling. Find your "sweet spot" – where God wants you. Serve God with a smile. Reflect His goodness as you touch the lives of others. Model the joy of serving God, and feel the fulfillment as you motivate others to action. Become a magnet for ministry movement.

> *"It's what God does with your life as he sets it right, puts it together, and completes it with joy. Your task is to single-mindedly serve Christ. Do that and you'll kill two birds with one stone: pleasing the God above you and proving your worth to the people around you."*
>
> *Romans 14:17b-18 (The Message)*

#61 Gone Fishin' Theme: Action

Are you living your faith?

Ever find yourself *talking* about advancing the Christian mission but *doing* little about it? We're called to be fishers of men and women, not keepers of the aquarium. Scripture says faith without action is dead. Beyond talking the talk, is it time to walk the walk and run the race? Faith leads to action. Of course, sit in church and attend Bible study. However, mission begins when you get out of your seat, onto your feet, and into the street. That is where you live your faith. God will use you to change the eternal destiny of others. Your personal mission field includes your friends, relatives, fellow workers, neighbors, and those at school. You carry their names on your phone.

Here's Our Prescription:

Schedule a few hours for quiet time with God. Spend time in Bible study and prayer. Is what you believe being translated into action? Are you satisfied with how you live out your faith? Ask God to help you. If you want to get your church moving for God, get yourself in gear. You can do this!

"Let your enthusiastic idea at the start be equaled by your realistic action now."
2 Corinthians 8:11b (The Living Bible)

#62 The God Box Theme: Action

Are you compartmentalized?

To those at church, Debbie appears to be a devout Christian. She worships regularly and attends a Bible class. During the week, she doesn't act like a scoundrel. Yet, she doesn't live with a God-consciousness. Lately, Debbie has been wondering: "How can my faith become a daily walk, instead of a weekly visit?"

Have you ever wondered about that? It is easy to get into the habit of putting God in the "weekly worship box." Life is hectic, probably too hectic.

Here's Our Prescription:

Try this: Spend time *daily* with God. It takes discipline. That is why Jesus calls you a "disciple." Begin your day with Him so you are *God-conscious* right from the beginning. Start with prayer. Too busy? Multitask. Pray while you brush your teeth or drive to work. (Just don't close your eyes!) Spend time in the Bible every day. Don't read a lot. Read often. Think. Apply. Reflect. Allow God to speak to you. Hear Him call you to action. Take God out of the Sunday box and into your daily life.

"In the morning, LORD, you hear my voice; in the morning I lay my requests before you and wait expectantly."
Psalm 5:3 (New International Version)

#63 Please Pass the Salt Theme: Action

What is your flavor?

Ask yourself every day: Do you flavor your environment? Or, does it flavor you? You are called to be salt that flavors others. You are seasoning that changes the world, one person at a time, one day at a time. God says you are a light that penetrates the darkness in our world. Would you like to be brighter light and more flavorful salt?

Jesus doesn't expect you to do that by your own strength. It is not another job you have to do. It is more like getting out of His way. It is "letting go and letting God." This occurs when He is in you. It is all about letting Jesus take charge.

Here's Our Prescription:

Pray, every day. Ask Jesus to take charge of your life. Ask for help to get out of His way. Start right now. He wants to answer your prayer, power up the light, and pour on the salt.

"You're here to be salt-seasoning that brings out the God-flavors of this earth."
Matthew 5:13a (The Message)

#64 Rot-Free Fruit — Theme: Significance

Do you think your life doesn't make much difference?

My wife, Janet, buys bananas and sets them on the counter. If no one eats them, they turn brown and begin to rot. Then she has to throw them in the trash. They last about a week, and then they're gone. However, not all fruit rots.

In John 15, Jesus says you can produce fruit that lasts. It never rots, not in a hundred years. Not in eternity. You know what's amazing? It's available to you—when you are connected to Him. How special is that? How powerful!

Here's Our Prescription:

Read John 15. Listen to Jesus as He speaks to you about the potential joy for your life. Consider what that could mean for you. Reflect on your life. Share your faith story with others. When you do, you produce fruit that will last for eternity! By God's power, you can change lives for now and forever. Live connected to Jesus, and join the journey of eternal significance.

"...I chose you and sent you out to produce fruit, the kind of fruit that will last."
John 15:16a (Contemporary English Version)

#65 God's Best for You

Theme: Significance

What will outlast your life?

Ever wonder why you're living this day, in this decade, in this century? Do you feel like you are alive just to punch a clock at work? Or pay off the mortgage? Raise your kids? Or bring home a paycheck? Is your big goal to work toward retirement? Or, is there more? Do you have a *legacy mission*? Do you have a vision to do what will continue even after you're gone? Could you plant a tree knowing you will never live long enough to sit under its shade?

Here's Our Prescription:

Evaluate your life. How would God describe you? Consider your unique gifts, talents, and passions. Reflect on your life goals and dreams. Write out a personal mission statement: why it is you believe God put you on earth. Then, add a vision statement—what do you believe God *could* do through you? Be bold. Discover God's best for you. Focus on His plan for your life.

"Our goal is to measure up to God's plan for us..."
2 Corinthians 10:13b (The Living Bible)

#66 Eternal Investments

Theme: Significance

Are you committed to significance?

Guinness World Records tells about a man who has eaten six bicycles, four chandeliers, and one airplane! So, what do you think he will say when God asks him what he did with his life? "I ate an airplane"? Do you really think God will say, "Well done, good and faithful servant"?

Ask yourself: "What could I do that would have eternal impact?"

Here's Our Prescription:

Take a break. Pray. Read your Bible. Ask God to speak to you, personally. How has He uniquely designed you? Change your perspective. Two men were breaking rocks with sledgehammers. When asked what they were doing, one said, "I'm breaking rocks." The other said, "I'm building a cathedral." That guy had discovered eternal significance. What about you? What is God calling you to do?

"As Jesus was walking beside Sea of Galilee, he saw two brothers, Simon called Peter and his brother Andrew. They were casting a net into the lake; for they were fishermen. 'Come, follow me,' Jesus said, 'and I will send you out to fish for people.'"
Matthew 4:18-19 (New International Version)

#67 Second Career

Theme: Significance

Ever feel you want to do more?

My friend Doug was a successful doctor in his first career. He made a good living and impacted many lives. Then he became a medical missionary and impacted countless numbers of people for this life and for eternity. It was his second career. He once made a living. Then he made an eternal difference. He lived the American dream. Then he joined a heavenly adventure. Of course, everything you do, as a Christian, has eternal significance. Whether you realize it or not, you are on a spiritual adventure.

Here's Our Prescription:

Discover more about how God has created you. What makes you unique? Learn about and develop your spiritual gifts. Get more involved at church. Let God speak to you through the experience. Take a retreat for Bible study and prayer. You may not be called to a foreign mission field. However, God does have a special plan for you.

"We can make our plans, but the LORD determines our steps."
Proverbs 16:9 (New Living Translation)

#68 Sight, with Vision

Theme: Significance

When you look into the mirror, what do you see?

When she was just one year old, Helen Keller became blind and deaf after a serious illness. She was once asked, "What could be worse than being blind?" She answered, "Having sight but no vision." Are you wrestling to discover God's future for you? If so, are you traveling down God's path for your destiny? Is it His plan for you? Have you discovered God's best for your future?

Here's Our Prescription:

God does have a plan for your life. If you seek Him, He will show it to you. Spend time in prayer. Not just today—every day. As you do, He will open doors. He will direct you, in His time. Even if you feel you are in the darkness, He will guide you. He will take your hand when everything seems cloudy. God knows your future. Ask Him to show you the way. You may not know what the future holds. But you will know He holds the future.

"'For I know the plans I have for you,' says the LORD. 'They are plans for good and not for disaster, to give you a future and a hope.'"
Jeremiah 29:11 (New Living Translation)

#69 Underwhelmed?

Theme: Significance

Are you bored?

Does life seem like a drudgery? Does it feel like there is no excitement? Do you lack motivation? Is it hard to get up in the morning? Perhaps you feel a lack of significance. Maybe you don't have a sense of direction or a clear view of the future. It is a common challenge. And, you are not alone. Yet, there is always hope on the horizon.

Here's Our Prescription:

Get clear on God's purpose. Read Scripture. Pray for guidance. It may require you move beyond focusing on yourself. Think about adding value to others. When you join God in what He is doing, you will end up on a spiritual adventure. It is often a wild ride, an exciting journey, and it always impacts eternity—in some way. Does that sound challenging? Yes! Stretching? For sure! But trust me, you will never be bored.

"...whoever does what God wants is set for eternity."
1 John 2:17b (The Message)

#70 Over the Cliff

Theme: Significance

Does life make sense?

One day, my friend Alan called to tell me that he had taken the week off work. He was praying, reading his Bible, and fasting. The next week he told me something I had prayed to hear: He decided to enter full-time ministry! "I'm over the cliff," he said. It doesn't make sense by human standards. But it makes all the sense in the world on the spiritual, eternal scale.

Perhaps you, too, are restless. Your day job no longer has value. You are searching for more fulfillment. Maybe you are feeling led to serve. But it doesn't make sense!

Here's Our Prescription:

Do what Alan did. Pray, fast, and read your Bible. Place yourself in God's care. Give your life to Him. He will put you in the right place. And guess what? It doesn't have to make sense. From a spiritual perspective, your heart will tell you what is right. Your Christian friends will confirm it.

"Just tell me what to do and I will do it, Lord. As long as I live I'll wholeheartedly obey."
Psalm 119:33-34 (The Living Bible)

#71 Hope Beyond the Grave — Theme: Death

Have you ever been to a cemetery?

Complete this statement: "Two things are sure, _____ and taxes." You got it! Death—it's a sure thing. It's hard to go to a funeral home and realize that someday the person lying there will be you. Even though people are living longer, we all die eventually. Does that send a chill down your spine?

That feeling is natural.

Here's Our Prescription:

Remember Jesus' words: "I am the resurrection and the life. Whoever believes in me, even though he dies, He will live." I don't know about you, but I think that is really great news! As a Christian, you can plan to die. Yet, you can also count on living again. And when you do, you will live like never before. You will be with Jesus. That makes your faith a source of great hope—even beyond the grave. Billy Graham said, "Death is not the end of life; it is only the gateway to eternity."

> *"'Where, Death, is your victory? Where, Death, is your power to hurt?' Death gets its power to hurt from sin, and sin gets its power from the Law. But thanks be to God who gives us the victory through our Lord Jesus Christ!"*
> *1 Corinthians 15:55-57 (Good News Translation)*

#72 The Grim Reaper? Theme: Death

Are you getting older?

On the positive side, each day is the first day of the rest of your life—filled with opportunity. But with every new day, you are one day closer to death. Every time you have a birthday, you are reminded about the passing of time. It's the truth—you won't live forever. Nobody does. Yet, that's not the whole truth.

Whoever made up the "Grim Reaper" must have been an unbeliever. What is so grim about death? Not so much for the believer in Christ. You know, there is something far greater on the other side. It is life with God: life without pain. Hope without despair. Love without hate. Life with Jesus! Life without end. I don't know about you, but I'm not having a "Grim Reaper" funeral. I want a joyous celebration.

Here's Our Prescription:

Perhaps it is time to plan your funeral. Plan a celebration. You can witness to your friends and family. It will be your last will and testimony!

"I've run hard right to the finish, believed all the way.
All that's left now is the shouting – God's applause!"
2 Timothy 4:7-8a (The Message)

#73 Plan to Die Theme: Death

Have you made a will?

A "last will and testament" basically directs what to do with your resources. It is a message to those you leave behind. Do you have a spiritual message for your heirs? Will you speak one more time? What about a funeral will? So many people die and their family has no idea how to make funeral arrangements. You have taken charge of your life. Now take charge of your last step.

Here's Our Prescription:

Help those you leave behind. Design a funeral will. Do it now! Share your favorite Bible verse. Tell them what songs, if any, you would like them to sing. You can make a video and give one last Christian witness to your relatives and friends. It might be your most powerful message. Think of the opportunities! Think of how you can help your family during their time of mourning. Your funeral could be a great occasion. Make a plan!

"For I am certain that nothing can separate us from his love: neither death nor life,…there is nothing in all creation that will ever be able to separate us from the love of God which is ours through Christ Jesus our Lord."
Romans 8:38a; 39b (Good News Translation)

#74 Don't Face Death Alone

Theme: Death

Are you feeling all alone?

Have you had a death in the family? It is a devastating experience. Even for those who believe in eternal life, it is a shock. It feels traumatic. Why would anybody want to go through that alone? Even if you are the only one left in your family—you should have your church family. You shouldn't have to bury a loved one alone—ever.

Here's Our Prescription:

Don't go through the death of someone close without the support of your church. The church is a community of believers. Christians understand pain, but they also celebrate real hope in Jesus Christ. Unbelievers come to the funeral home and say, "George sure looks nice." No, he doesn't. He's dead! Compare that to, "I'm sorry for your loss. You are in our prayers." We are all going to face the death of someone we love. The good news is, as God's people, we don't have to face it alone.

"Christ is like a single body, which has many parts; it is still one body, even though it is made up of different parts.... If one part of the body suffers, all the other parts suffer with it.... All of you are Christ's body, and each one is a part of it."
1 Corinthians 12:12, 26a, 27 (Good News Translation)

#75 What Are Your Thoughts? Theme: Death

Do you think about death much?

Have you been with someone at their moment of death? If not, you might think it's scary. Actually, there's something wondrous about it. There is a release, a peace. If you feel ambivalent about death, you are not alone. In truth, everyone eventually ponders their own last moment on earth.

Jesus died, but rose again. And He promised to bring every believer with Him, through the same process: both death and resurrection. Someone once said, "If your head is in heaven, you don't have to be afraid to put your feet in the grave."

Here's Our Prescription:

In your thoughts about death, remember John 3:16: "For God loved the world so much that He sent His only Son. Whoever believes in Him will not die but have eternal life." As a believer in Christ, you can ponder your death in peace.

"I am, right now, Resurrection and Life. The one who believes in me, even though he or she dies, will live. And everyone who lives believing in me does not ultimately die at all…."
John 11:25b-26 (The Message)

#76 Calamity Events — Theme: Death

Are you prepared for an emergency?

It seems like ancient history. In 1999, many thought the world would shut down. They called it Y2K. However, the nightmare never occurred. Some stocked up with food. Others learned survival tactics. The same fears occurred on 9/11 when terrorists attacked New York's Twin Towers and the Pentagon in Washington, D.C. Mass shootings, out-of-control wildfires, ISIS attacks, COVID-19: All get our attention. Horrific events teach an important lesson: Calamity clarifies.

In calamity, you discover real priorities. You learn about your character. Are you prepared to help others in times of crisis? It could be a natural disaster, death in the family, or a long-term illness.

Here's Our Prescription:

In challenging times, people are most receptive to good news about Jesus. See challenges as spiritual opportunities. Let your Christian character shine. Your compassion and your faith are powerful witnesses. Calamity clarifies eternity, even to you.

"There is wonderful joy ahead, even though the going is rough for a while down here."
1 Peter 1:6b (The Living Bible)

#77 Card Ministry Theme: Death

Do you care about those who grieve?

There is a proverb that says, "It takes a thousand positive words to overcome a negative one." Words are powerful, especially during seasons of grief. This is a great ministry you could pioneer. Commit yourself to monitoring those who have lost a loved one.

Here's Our Prescription:

Send an email, text, or even a card. In our world of electronic communication, a card in the mail stands out more than ever. You don't have to know them well. Track down their address. Send a Christian card. You can send it on behalf of your church. Let them know they are in your prayers. Give them your church's phone number and offer further care. Reach out when they may need it most. Start a card ministry, and see how many people you impact! A card, and your thoughtfulness, can communicate God's great power in life and death.

"God will strengthen you with his own great power so that you will not give up when troubles come, but you will be patient."
Colossians 1:11 (New Century Version)

#78 Wanted, Not Needed Theme: Service

Yes, that's you!

Have you ever seen one of those old posters that says, "Uncle Sam Needs You!" Well, here is a revelation: God does *not* need you. God doesn't need anybody. However, He does *want* you. He wants you to be involved. He invites you to share in the most joyful dimension of the human experience—being a part of what He's doing in the lives of others.

Here's Our Prescription:

Find your ministry. Every Christian is a "minister." By God's design, every Christian is called to serve in some capacity. Church is not a spectator arena or a spiritual restaurant where you are divinely fed. It is a boot camp, a launchpad for mission. We gather so we can be scattered. So, find your calling and your mission. You are wanted by the Ruler of the universe. Find your ministry and discover miraculous fulfillment!

"People come up and tell us how you…deserted the dead idols of your old life so you could embrace and serve God, the true God."
1 Thessalonians 1:9 (The Message)

#79 Frightened? Theme: Service

Are you scared?

Marcy was asked to serve in a ministry to reach children in the community. She was honored to be chosen, excited about the possibilities—and scared to death. Ever find yourself petrified by the awesome opportunity of serving Almighty God?

Here's Our Prescription:

Cut yourself a little slack. And give God a little credit. First of all, you don't change the lives of others. God does. He honors you by calling you an ambassador for Jesus Christ. The Apostle Paul said, "It is not me, but Christ in me." God will work through you as you serve. Your job is to listen to His direction, follow His lead, and get out of His way! He will do the rest!

"I can do all things through Christ who strengthens me."
Philippians 4:13 (New King James Version)

#80 Challenges - with Help! Theme: Service

Do you have challenges?

Three boys were arguing about whose dad was richest. One said, "My dad's a doctor." The second boy said, "My dad's richer. He's a banker." The third boy said, "My dad's an elder at church. He's so rich he owns hell." "How do you know that?" asked his friend. The boy replied, "Because he said at the church council meeting last week, they gave it to him!"

In all seriousness—Christian service can be hard. Look at anyone in Scripture, including Jesus. They all experienced challenges.

Here's Our Prescription:

Believe God's promise: He will never give you more than you can handle—with His help. Seek Him every day, and do what Scripture says: "Be strong and unmovable." In truth? It is the way most ministry gets done!

> *"We had just been given rough treatment…but that didn't slow us down…. God tested us thoroughly to make sure we were qualified to be trusted with this Message…. We're not after crowd approval – only God approval."*
> *1 Thessalonians 2:2-4 (The Message)*

#81 You Are Gifted Theme: Service

Did you know? You are supernaturally gifted!

Martin got up to speak before the congregation. To be honest, it was awful. It was clear: Public speaking is not his gift. However, I was with Martin when we met with a family who had visited our church. In their living room, he shared about Jesus—in a powerful way! Martin is no public speaker, but he does have the gift to witness his faith!

Do you know which gifts the Holy Spirit has given uniquely to you?

Here's Our Prescription:

Take a spiritual gifts survey. Share the results with a Christian friend who knows you well. Pray for guidance. Learn what Scripture says about your gifts. Discover where God wants you to serve. Spiritual gifts are the Holy Spirit's way of organizing the church. And it works! Your gifts reveal God's plan for your life!

"Since we have gifts that differ according to the grace given to us, each of us is to exercise them accordingly…"
Romans 12:6 (New American Standard Bible)

#82 The Least Theme: Service

Are you reaching out?

A man picked up a hitchhiker wearing only one shoe. He asked, "What happened to your other shoe?" The man replied, "I only found one." Sometimes, human nature leads us to focus on the negative. Do you look for the worst instead of the best in others? Jesus always looked for the best.

So, what is your attitude toward those who are less fortunate? Do you see them as "your neighbor" here on earth? Jesus did. Are they worthy of your compassion? Would it be spiritually appropriate to identify their needs and help them?

Here's Our Prescription:

Touch the "untouchables." Love the "unlovables." Do what Jesus would do. You will receive more than you ever give. Make a list of those you know to whom you could be the hands and feet of Jesus.

"The King will reply, 'I tell you, whenever you did this for one of the least important of these followers of mine, you did for me!'"
Matthew 25:40 (Good News Translation)

#83 Give and Take Theme: Service

Are you balanced?

In the Holy Land, Lake Galilee receives water from the Jordan River. The lake is healthy and vibrant, supporting the surrounding villages. From there, the water flows into the Dead Sea, where it stops. There is no outlet. It receives water, but does not pass it on. And it *is* dead.

If all you do is receive from God, but never give it to others, you end up spiritually constipated. Healthy Christians are balanced believers. You receive so much from God. However, you get "out of balance" unless you also serve and give. This is why God wants to cultivate your passion for mission and service. A mission mentality multiplies spiritual life. You become an ambassador for Christ. So, are you balanced?

Here's Our Prescription:

Take what you get from God, and turn it into giving to others. What would happen to your world if you lived that balance?

"So we are ambassadors for Christ, God making his appeal through us."
2 Corinthians 5:20a (Revised Standard Version)

#84 The Significance Adventure — Theme: Service

Are you signed up?

John is a successful businessman whose life is full but without adventure. He doesn't need money or fame. Yet, he wants to be a part of something exciting. He desires something bigger than himself. What is he really missing? Involvement in a ministry gets his spiritual blood pumping.

When you work with God, you join an eternal enterprise. Jesus said when you connect with Him, you produce *much* fruit. The joy of Jesus is injected into your life. Your joy is complete. You experience supernatural fulfillment.

Here's Our Prescription:

Join the adventure! Help others to join you. It will change your life—and theirs. It will change your church. And your church will change this world, one person at a time. Take the initiative—sign up!

"...my dear, dear friends, stand your ground. And don't hold back. Throw yourselves into the work of the Master, confident that nothing you do for him is a waste of time or effort."
1 Corinthians 15:58 (The Message)

#85 Endangered Pastors Theme: Pastors

Can you help?

Management expert Peter Drucker once said, "The clergy are the most discouraged professionals …." Today, pastors have two choices: (1) Don't rock the boat and watch the church decline, or (2) lead change—which upsets some of the members. How is that for an exciting career?

It is a tough time to be a pastor. At the rate churches are losing pastors, they might become an endangered species! So, how can you help?

Here's Our Prescription:

Make this your personal mission: Speak a word of encouragement to your pastor at every opportunity. Encourage others in your church to do the same. That little gift of encouragement can go a long way! Hey, we need our pastors! Be determined to help get your pastor off the endangered list! And, whatever your career, could God be calling you to full-time ministry?

"Appreciate your pastoral leaders who gave you the Word of God."
Hebrews 13:7 (The Message)

#86 Your Growing Pastor Theme: Pastors

Are you helping your pastor grow?

Leading a church is challenging. God's truth remains the same, but everything else in our world is changing. It is a tough time to lead a church effectively. It is really important for pastors to learn how to reach unbelievers. However, with crowded schedules and shrinking budgets, pastors often sacrifice crucial opportunities to learn. Many find personal and professional growth are not options. Yet, it is essential, especially in the area of strategic ways to reach the lost.

Here's Our Prescription:

Be a champion! Help your pastor become a lifelong learner. Provide finances for your pastor to get resources that provide encouragement and help. If your pastor wants to attend a conference, encourage church members to raise the funds. Help your pastor to learn and lead. Pastors either grow—or go away. You can make the difference! And, it will help your church to grow—not go away.

"...continue to grow in the grace and knowledge of our Lord and Savior Jesus Christ."
2 Peter 3:18 (Good News Translation)

#87 The Pastor's Spouse Theme: Pastors

Who stands behind your pastor?

Serving as a pastor today is one of life's toughest callings. However, the greater challenge often falls to the pastor's "pastor" — the pastor's spouse. I have met many strong pastors backed by healthy spouses. I have seen troubled pastors with less supportive spouses.

Some pastors' mates are lonely and discouraged. They may even be angry about what they perceive the church is doing to the person they love. What can you do to help?

Here's Our Prescription:

You can start a movement to give special attention to the pastor's spouse. Keep pastors and their spouses in your prayers. Provide special gifts. Become a spiritual friend. Be a champion for time off and spiritual growth. Show you really care. Give encouragement — it will go a long way! If you love your church, love your pastor.

"Friends love through all kinds of weather, and families stick together in all kinds of trouble."
Proverbs 17:17 (The Message)

#88 They Cry, Too Theme: Pastors

Do you hear it?

I once read a book about pastors with the title *They Cry, Too*. It described how many pastors—hurt by their congregations—felt they have nowhere to turn. They suffer alone. I often work with dysfunctional churches. Sometimes the issues are wrongfully blamed on the pastor. It is sad when the person who helps everyone else can't get help when it is needed most.

You can be a decisive force of encouragement for your pastor.

Here's Our Prescription:

Be there with Christian love and integrity. Why wouldn't you want to help? Pastors aren't robots! They are human. Their feelings are real. They cry, too. If you can be there for them, they can be there for you. Start a Pastor's Family Care Team. A church committed to loving the pastor will more effectively impact the world for Jesus.

"Do not be overcome by evil, but overcome evil with good."
Romans 12:21 (New International Version)

#89 Prayer Pillar — Theme: Pastors

Are you a pillar?

A pastor was late for the church supper. So, Joe led the prayer: "As there is no pastor present, let us give thanks to the Lord!" Whoops! Every church has pillars and caterpillars. The pillars hold up ministry. The caterpillars just crawl in and out. Consider this: You could be a prayer pillar of support for your pastor and for the leaders of the church.

Here's Our Prescription:

If you are thankful for the pastor and church leaders, pray for them every day. Let them know you are praying. Ask them about their prayer needs. Check with them later to see if your prayers have been answered. You can make a difference! Your prayers are powerful! Church leaders need prayer pillars!

"...pray with holy hands lifted up to God, free from anger and controversy."
1 Timothy 2:8 (New Living Translation)

#90 Part of the Solution Theme: Pastors

Do you ever say, "Oops?"

When I was a young pastor, I was afraid of making mistakes. I knew I wasn't perfect. It frightened me. An older, seasoned pastor put his arm around me and said, "We serve under the shadow of the cross." He was right. We all depend on grace. We don't deserve it. It is a gift. Our mistakes? They are all forgivable.

Here's Our Prescription:

When your pastor makes a mistake, remember what Jesus taught about taking the log out of your own eye before you get all hung up about the speck in others'—even your pastor's. Make this commitment: "I'm going to be a part of my pastor's success, not failure." Don't be part of the problem. Remember, at one time your pastor was a baby with a messy diaper. So were you! So, be part of the solution. Turn mistakes into opportunities.

"Why, then, do you look at the speck in your brother's eye and pay no attention to the log in your own eye? How dare you say to your brother, 'Please, let me take that speck out of your eye,' when you have a log in your own eye? You hypocrite! First take the log out of your own eye, and then you will be able to see clearly to take the speck out of your brother's eye."
Matthew 7:3-5 (Good News Translation)

#91 The Pastor's Purpose Theme: Pastors

"Alexa, play piano music!"

Your pastor is not an electronic gadget waiting for you to bark orders. A farmer entered his mule in the Kentucky Derby. He said, "I didn't think he'd win, but I thought the association would do him a world of good." Jesus understood the value of leading others and equipping them for ministry. He said, "Come follow me and I will make you fishers of men" (Matthew 4:19). Jesus reflects a high view of people who can do extraordinary things. He sees you as a winner. Do you pray for your pastor?

Here's Our Prescription:

Do you see your pastor as a "hired hand"? Ephesians 4 says pastors *equip God's people to do the work of ministry*. Pastors are coaches. Their job is not primarily to do ministry, but to disciple people like you to do ministry. Ministry to others is a privilege and a joy. You can help your pastor, and your church, become more effective than ever! Ask your pastor and leaders to disciple you. Multiply! It's God's divine design. That way, everyone wins.

"He (Christ) handed out gifts of apostle, prophet, evangelist, and pastor-teacher to train Christ's followers in skilled servant work, working within Christ's body, the church…."
Ephesians 4:11-12 (The Message)

#92 The "S" Word Theme: Sacrifice

Are you afraid to say it?

Dawn and Marcia were talking about their friend, Darlene. "I don't understand why she spends so much time at church. It seems like she doesn't have any time for herself." "I don't know," replied Marcia, "but she is really happy doing what she does, don't you think?"

Ever wonder why some people get involved in ministry and others never step up? In many cases, it boils down to how they view church. Do you think of "sacrifice" as a foreign or nasty word? A negative thing?

Here's Our Prescription:

Sacrifice is a biblical concept. The road to any significant achievement includes sacrifice. You have likely heard it: "No pain, no gain!" Working for God does have rewards: spiritual growth, fulfillment, and adventure. So, don't be afraid of sacrifice. It could be your gateway to eternal joy that is out of this world. Yet, it improves this world.

"May the God of peace provide you with every good thing you need in order to do his will, and may he, through Jesus Christ, do in us what pleases him. And to Christ be the glory forever and ever!"
Hebrews 13:21 (Good News Translation)

#93 What's Negotiable? Theme: Sacrifice

How do you decide?

During worship, Pastor John announced, "The homeless shelter is looking for Christian helpers to cook and clean." It was amazing to look around the worship center. Almost everyone took their eyes off the pastor and looked at the floor! It does happen: God will give you opportunities to serve. Are you ready?

Here's Our Prescription:

Think about your "negotiables." How much time and energy are you willing to set aside? Budget your time. What do you have to give? What are your gifts? In that context, look for opportunities to serve. It may *feel like a sacrifice.* Prepare spiritually: If God calls, you will serve. Now you are prepared when God calls on you. Remember, most people miss the joy of sacrifice. Why? Spiritual growth opportunities come disguised as hard work!

"God in his mercy has given us this work to do, and so we do not become discouraged."
2 Corinthians 4:1 (Good News Translation)

#94 What Wouldn't You Do? Theme: Sacrifice

Are you ready for anything?

Perhaps you have heard about the housekeeper who says, "I don't do windows." Have you ever thought about what you are *unwilling* to do—for God? What if Noah had said, "I don't build boats"? Or, what if Moses responded, "I don't do wilderness trips"? What if Jesus reflected, "I don't do crosses"?

Here's Our Prescription:

Focus on what you *are willing to do* for God. Could your unwillingness be a wrong turn on a journey where God wants to take you? I invited Laura to join our team to serve in the Amazon jungle. After the shock, she said, "Yes!" It changed her life. In fact, she went back again! So, give your life over to God—all of it. And watch, with excitement, where God might take you! Isn't that what faith is all about? What could happen if there was *nothing* you wouldn't to do for God? Spiritual adventure is often disguised as sacrifice!

"For I have come down from heaven to do the will of God who sent me, not to do my own will." – Jesus
John 6:38 (New Living Translation)

#95 What's Nonnegotiable? Theme: Sacrifice

Do you have boundaries?

Poor Fred. He is the church treasurer, a Sunday school teacher, a trustee, and a deacon. And, Fred is at the point where he dreads going to church! Either he feels like he's really committed—or ought to be (to some institution!). Are you a Fred? Do you need to focus?

When it comes to God's work, there is *always* more work to do. If you don't have boundaries, you can't have balance. Without balance, you fall. You can be on fire. You can also burn out.

Here's Our Prescription:

Determine the limits of your time and energy. Then determine your nonnegotiables. What is it that you won't sacrifice? Find your nonnegotiables, and you will know when to say, "No." In the long run, you become more helpful to God. You don't have to die for your church. Jesus already did. So, find your focus, and maximize your potential for God.

"...we should choose to follow what is right. But first of all we must define...what is good."
Job 34:4 (The Living Bible)

#96 Loose Change and Leftovers? Theme: Sacrifice

Do you sacrificially give finances for God's work?

A man was about to be baptized in a river. Suddenly, he ran out of the water, saying he forgot to remove his wallet. The preacher stopped him: "Come back with the wallet. I've got too many unbaptized wallets in my congregation already."

Do you have a "baptized" bank account? Giving to God's work is not about *loose* change and *extra* time. It is *sacrificial* giving, by faith. It doesn't depend on your resources or ability to give. It depends on God, who calls you to sacrifice. Why would He do that? So He can demonstrate faithfulness in you, and you can show trust in Him.

So, is what you give to God a sacrifice? Does it impact your lifestyle? Does it adjust your "want" list? Or is it, for you, just "leftovers" for God?

Here's Our Prescription:

Trust the Lord. Give until it hurts. Learn that you can't outgive God. Experience the miracle of generosity. Discover that you never felt so good!

> *"Give away your life; you'll find life given back, but not merely given back – given back with bonus and blessing. Giving, not getting, is the way. Generosity begets generosity."*
> *Luke 6:38 (The Message)*

#97 Tip or Tithe? Theme: Sacrifice

What is the difference?

I saw Art sitting alone in the restaurant. He is "Mr. Grouch." I sat with him anyway. He complained about the pastor's preaching on tithing: "The preacher wants us to give ten percent. An offering begins with eleven percent. It's just too much for those on a fixed income." As we left, he gave a fifteen percent tip to the waitress.

What is the difference between a tip and a tithe? A tip shows gratitude for service. A tithe returns to God a portion of what is *already His*. It is an act of faith. Sacrifice in this world celebrates the next. Missionary Jim Elliot was martyred. Before he died, he said, "He is no fool who gives up what he cannot keep in order to gain what he cannot lose."

Here's Our Prescription:

Sacrifice! Honestly, you can't lose! Live, love, and give generously to God!

> *"Remember: A stingy planter gets a stingy crop; a lavish planter gets a lavish crop. I want each of you to take plenty of time to think it over, and make up your own mind what you will give. That will protect you against sob stories and arm-twisting. God loves it when the giver delights in the giving."*
> *2 Corinthians 9:6-7 (The Message)*

#98 Working for God — Theme: Sacrifice

Who do you work for?

I spend a lot of time on airplanes. To make the best use of my time, I work while I'm flying. On one occasion, the man next to me saw my pile of papers and said, "You work too hard." I replied, "I love working for God." And I do! Being a Church Doctor has required many sacrifices, but they are more than worth it.

Before Jesus ascended into heaven, He said, "GO!" That means: until He says "STOP!" As long as you live, there will be an assignment for you. It may require sacrifice. It could change the way you live your life.

Here's Our Prescription:

If He calls you to serve, to give, to sacrifice, be thankful! Be honored! Be willing! When He calls, take a deep breath, thank Him for the assignment, and get ready to go! Don't ever allow sacrifice to stop you. Jesus didn't!

"So here's what I want you to do, God helping you: Take your everyday, ordinary life – your sleeping, eating, going-to-work, and walking-around life – and place it before God as an offering."
Romans 12:1 (The Message)

#99 Share the Load, Win the World — Theme: Team

Are you working with others?

John Maxwell says, "Teamwork makes the dream work." Teamwork divides the work, but multiplies the impact. God's plan for believers is a multiplication strategy. It is designed as teamwork. Why, then, do many Christians resist? Perhaps some don't get the plan. Are you one of them?

Here's Our Prescription:

Ask yourself: What holds you back? What stops you from working with others on God's team? The missionary Robert Morrison said, "The great fault in our missions is that nobody likes to be second." Is that your challenge? Or, are you willing to share the success? Can you set your pride aside and share the load with others? In sports, it takes the whole team to win the game. In God's work, it takes the whole team to win the world.

"By yourself you're unprotected. With a friend you can face the worst. Can you round up a third? A three-stranded rope isn't easily snapped."
Ecclesiastes 4:12 (The Message)

#100 Generational Parts Theme: Team

Can you involve your children or grandchildren in ministry?

When our son was young, every few weeks, the worship team at church included him on the drums. His friend was occasionally asked to play guitar. Another girl their age would sing. They even had a young adult who would give the message. Were they as good as the adults? No, not yet. They were being trained and mentored. They were being discipled.

Here's Our Prescription:

It is a mistake to think Christian ministry is reserved for adults. Or, for that matter, only "seasoned" church members. Or, worse, only for "professionals." Ministry is the privilege of every believer in Christ. At a conference, I saw a girl, about ten years old, serving pizza at lunch. Was she wondering if she is qualified to serve? Not likely! God invites you to advance the Kingdom among everyone—whether they are young, old, or in between. So, if you are older, what can you do to encourage those who are younger? If you are younger, what could you do to remind older folks? Everyone should have the opportunity to serve the Lord. It takes everybody to be the body of Christ! What will you do?

"All of you are Christ's body, and each one is a part of it."
1 Corinthians 12:27 (Good News Translation)

#101 Retirement Theme: Team

Do you need to be reenergized?

Satchel Paige said, "Age is just mind over matter. If you don't mind, it doesn't matter." But your life does matter—to God. And, it is supposed to matter for God! Instead of being retired, consider getting refired. Many people have contributed greatly after the age of so-called "retirement." My mentor was the late Donald McGavran. He was past retirement when he launched a school of missions. That school has influenced churches around the world. It changed my life. My life has changed many others.

Here's Our Prescription:

Perhaps you are not near retirement. Then think of your parents or grandparents. Invite them to engage in work that has eternal consequences. Fulfillment in God's work is spiritual fuel for life. So, get out of that armchair and get on the team. You do matter to God! And, as you bless others, you will be blessed! The more you serve God, the younger you feel. Feel the joy!

"Serve the LORD with gladness!"
Psalm 100:2a (Revised Standard Version)

#102 The Jesus Workout Theme: Team

Are you ready to sweat?

It's a twenty-first century phenomenon: Couch Potato. He is a cousin to Armchair Quarterback, cousin to Lazy Boy Louie, married to Spectator Susie. Yet, God still loves these people. That's good, because you may be one of them.

Christianity is not a spectator sport. It takes focus. It requires discipline—as in "disciple." That is how faith gets stronger. In sports, they call it a "workout"—as in *work*.

Here's Our Prescription:

Here's a plan for spiritual exercise. Pray every day. Read your Bible. Discover your spiritual gifts. Get involved. Be a part of the team. Roll up your sleeves—there's work to do! Get off your ecclesiastical backside, get out of your comfort zone, get on your feet, go out in the street, and make a difference in this world. It will be good for you! It is healthy for your church. It is great for our world. It is called a Jesus workout! Discover *real* joy!

> *"So let's keep focused on that goal, those of us who want everything God has for us. If any of you have something else in mind, something less than total commitment, God will clear your blurred vision—you'll see it yet! Now that we're on the right track, let's stay on it."*
>
> *Philippians 3:15-16 (The Message)*

#103 Benchwarmers Theme: Team

Are you sitting this one out?

When I played high school football, I tried to become a running back, but was too slow. I tried tight end, but couldn't catch the ball! I spent most of my time on the bench. Then the coach suggested I try defensive end. I found my place!

Are you a benchwarmer at church? Are you not getting in "the game" of ministry because you haven't found where you fit? Maybe you are in the wrong position. Many people pick areas to serve based on where their friends are, or where others expect them to be. That is not God's approach. You are not a volunteer. God has called you to serve.

Here's Our Prescription:

Let your spiritual gifts lead you to your place of ministry. If you don't know what they are, take a spiritual gifts survey. The Holy Spirit has put you in this world for a specific ministry. There are no benchwarmers on team Jesus! Losing is not an option. God has recruited you so He can win—the world!

"As each has received a gift, employ it for one another, as good stewards of God's varied grace...."
1 Peter 4:10 (Revised Standard Version)

#104 Make the Most of Meetings

Theme: Team

Are you tired of meetings?

In John 3:16, the Scripture could have said, "For God so loved the world that He did not send a committee." Is your Christian life bogged down by bureaucracy? It's like that church board. They all died in a fire. No one could figure out Robert's Rules of Order to adjourn the meeting! Many Christians suffer from death by meetings.

Here's Our Prescription:

If you are on a church committee, add spiritual vitality to your team. Spend time in prayer. Find out what is going on in each other's spiritual lives. Share what God is doing in your life. Ask the Holy Spirit to set your agenda. Set measurable goals. Take direction from Scripture. Let your passion drive the work. Celebrate progress, and thank the Lord. Have fun!

"Rather, speaking the truth in love, we are to grow up in every way into him who is the head, into Christ, from whom the whole body, joined and knit together by every joint with which it is supplied, when each part is working properly, makes bodily growth and upbuilds itself in love."
Ephesians 4:15-16 (Revised Standard Version)

#105 Teamwork Triumph Theme: Team

Trying to do too much alone?

Someone once said, "Nothing is impossible for people who don't have to do it all themselves." Every significant accomplishment in history has been the result of teamwork. In fact, this book you are holding involved a team.

What dream is God putting on your heart? What challenge or endeavor would radically change the lives of those around you? If God sends you on a mission, you want a team to help.

Here's Our Prescription:

Don't try to serve God alone. Share the vision God gives you. Get help from others who will invest in the dream. Watch God work through your team. If Jesus is your Captain, your team has eternal significance.

"When Jethro saw everything that Moses had to do, he asked, 'What is all this that you are doing for the people? Why are you doing this all alone...? You will wear yourself out and these people as well. This is too much for you to do alone...you should choose some capable men and appoint them as leaders of the people...."

Exodus 18:14a, 18, 21a (Good News Translation)

#106 Anticipate the Positive Theme: Attitude

Do you feel trapped?

We see it all the time in churches we consult. Some believers are discouraged. Others are dejected or pessimistic. Are you one of them? Jesus was in the Garden of Gethsemane—facing a horrible death. Do you think—even momentarily—He was wondering if there was another way? God is more interested in your character than your comfort. Challenging times are usually growth opportunities.

Life gets tough, even for Christians.

Here's Our Prescription:

Take a deep breath, say a prayer, and face this reality: Sometimes, you can't do much about what happens to you. However, you can always choose how you react. Turn to God, and trust this: He is always in control. Anticipate the positive. Even through challenges, you are likely to grow in your faith. Ask God for strength. Focus on His love. Celebrate His promises. Let God encourage you!

"But God, who encourages those who are discouraged, encouraged us...."
2 Corinthians 7:6 (New Living Translation)

#107 Morning Glory Theme: Attitude

Is it, for you, a *good* morning?

There is a test to determine if you are a "morning person." Instead of exclaiming, "Good morning, Lord!" do you ever say, "Oh Lord, is it morning already?" If so, that may not be the best way to start your day! Get up with this in mind: Every day, you have a divine purpose. As a believer, you are on a mission for the Ruler of the universe.

Here's Our Prescription:

Spend your first waking moments repeating this prayer: "Lord, use me this day." I've done that for years. And, all that God has done blows my mind! What if you are *not* a morning person? To help you remember, put a note on your phone or on the bathroom mirror: "Lord, use me today." Then watch! See what God does with your day. It could change your life. God will change your attitude. And through you, God will change the world. He will change you, whether you are a "morning person" or not!

"Surprise us with love at daybreak; then we'll skip and dance all the day long."
Psalm 90:14 (The Message)

#108 Attitude and Fruit Theme: Attitude

What do you think? Is that an apple or a peach?

During winter, it's hard to tell an apple tree from a peach tree—both are bare. You really learn about the nature of a tree by seeing its fruit. Ever think about God's attitude toward you? You can't see His attitude. You can't measure it. But you can see the fruit.

Here's Our Prescription:

Read Philippians 2:1-11. It describes the attitude of Jesus. Humble. Obedient. More interested in you than in Himself. Philippians 2:5 says you can have an attitude just like His—an outlook shaped by Him. This could change the fruit of your life. Do you think that would make a difference among your friends? In your church? What about in our world? You can be certain: It would!

"Your attitude should be the kind that was shown us by Jesus Christ...."
Philippians 2:5 (The Living Bible)

#109 The Difference That Makes the Difference — Theme: Attitude

What shapes your attitude?

Ever notice that some athletes really soar? Others, sooner or later, just seem to fall apart or get in trouble. Why is that? Their athletic abilities might be fantastic, but what ultimately shapes their level of success—or failure—is their attitude.

That is true for you, too. Have you ever felt sorry you did what you did, thought what you thought, said what you said? It's not really what you did, thought, or said. It is more about what is going on inside. Your attitude drives your behavior. What is the *altitude* of your attitude?

Here's Our Prescription:

Spend quiet time with God. Do it every day. Pray for God's attitude to grow inside of you. When you have a God attitude, it impacts your behavior. Your faith—and your life—will soar! The more God directs your life, the more your faith grows. The more your faith grows, the more God directs your life!

"Be careful how you think; your life is shaped by your thoughts."
Proverbs 4:23 (Good News Translation)

#110 Churchitude Theme: Attitude

Are you bummed out?

You hear your church is doing away with the 9 a.m. service. It's your favorite. Your pastor has good reasons for doing it, but it messes up your schedule. It requires you to change, and change makes you uncomfortable. Think about the old light bulb joke: "How many church members does it take to change a light bulb? *Who said anything about change?"*

Are you upset about something at church right now?

Here's Our Prescription:

Don't get angry. Give it some time. Don't talk negatively to others. Talk to your leaders. Learn more about why they made the change. Listen with the desire to understand. Develop a constructive plan about how you will react to the discomfort you feel. Pray, asking God to guide you and to give you a good attitude. Your attitude can spread to others who might be struggling. Look to Jesus. He will give you victory, even over bad attitudes.

"You are only hurting yourself with your anger."
Job 18:4a (Good News Translation)

#111 Attitude Altitude   Theme: Attitude

Is your attitude soaring or crashing?

I find this among some church members everywhere I go: negative attitudes. And why not? Christians are human. We get tired. We have health challenges. We experience disappointments. We get temporarily discouraged. Right?

So, what do you do when you feel down and out?

Here's Our Prescription:

Pray. Ask God for a better attitude. Ask Him to bless your boss, help your job situation, improve your approach to your kids, or improve your attitude about school. No matter what your challenge, God cares. My son played basketball. After one of their games, he didn't think his team played very well. I suggested he pray for each of his team members. He did it, and you know what? They not only improved, but perhaps more importantly, so did he—especially his attitude! Prayer works on the basketball court, at school, with your children, or at work. God can change your attitude anywhere in life. When your spiritual attitude rises, everyone wins.

"Don't just pretend to love others. Really love them. Hate what is wrong. Hold tightly to what is good."
Romans 12:9 (New Living Translation)

#112 How You See the Glass Theme: Attitude

Are you up—or down?

Last night, my wife and I went to dinner at one of our favorite restaurants. When we got home, I said, "Wasn't that a great supper?" She said, "Yes, but it was a little expensive." Then I thought—why look at the downside? She knew what I was thinking. We laughed. Does that ever happen to you? Do you see the glass half empty instead of half full?

The Bible says, in everything, God works for good for those who love Him. My wife knows that. It's likely you do as well. Yet, we all have our moments, right?

Here's Our Prescription:

When you are discouraged, remember: God is—God. He is in control. You can trust Him. With God, you have help. Focus on the glass half full. Let God's power transform you into an *optimistic* believer. Try looking at every problem as a challenge, every challenge as an opportunity, every opportunity as a possibility. Call it the T.J.S. approach: Think Jesus Saves. If He can do that, He can fill your glass to overflowing.

"And we know that in all things God works for the good of those who love him, who have been called according to his purpose."
Romans 8:28 (New International Version)

#113 Fallen

Theme: Mistakes

Have you fallen?

A man with a Bible was reading in a park. Some people nearby began making fun of him. "Hey," one shouted, "how far is it to heaven?" The man replied, "It's only one step, and God has already taken it." When Jesus came to earth, God took the first step.

It is amazing to know God forgives your sins. You aren't perfect—no one is. Have you noticed? Even if you follow Jesus and try to do the right thing, sometimes you make mistakes. We all do. How do you react?

Here's Our Prescription:

When you fall, tell God you're sorry. Then focus on God's amazing grace—the free gift of His love. Fall deeper in love with Jesus. Don't let mistakes keep you down. Let God pick you up! With God's forgiveness, you always fall forward. If you love Jesus, you are set free.

"God puts people right through their faith in Jesus Christ. God does this to all who believe in Christ, because there is no difference at all: everyone has sinned and is far away from God's saving presence. But by the free gift of God's grace all are put right with him through Christ Jesus, who sets them free."
Romans 3:22-24 (Good News Translation)

#114 Failuritis — Theme: Mistakes

Did you goof?

Football great Mike Ditka said, "You never really lose until you quit trying." A man by the name of Ben Jonson once said, "You don't really know your own strength until you have met adversity." What are they both saying? Don't give up! Failure is part of the price of success. The key isn't to run from it, but to embrace it.

You can learn a lot from a failure! It took Thomas Edison one thousand tries to invent the first light bulb! If he had given up on failure 999, you might still be in the dark.

Here's Our Prescription:

Don't fear failure. If you make a mistake, learn from it. Ask God to help you grow. It is not the end of the world if you fail. Yet, it is the end of opportunity if you quit. Never give up on God. Why? He will never give up on you! It is called GRACE: God's Riches at Christ's Expense.

"'...My grace is sufficient for you, for my power is made perfect in weakness.'"
2 Corinthians 12:9a (New International Version)

#115 Grow Up Inside — Theme: Mistakes

Are you growing every day?

In his book *The Prayer of Jabez*, Bruce Wilkinson wrote, "The deepest grief I've seen in fellow believers is among those who have experienced extraordinary blessings, territory, and power…only to slip into serious sin." No matter how long you have followed Jesus, or how blessed your life has been, you will always be tempted to sin. As long as you are breathing, you need God's forgiveness. You need to keep growing spiritually.

My friend Jerry says, "When I'm ninety, God will convict me of some sin and I'll say, 'Why didn't I learn that when I was eighty?'" Spiritual growth is a process—not an event. If you are spiritually wise, you will grow the rest of your life.

Here's Our Prescription:

Whatever you do, keep your focus on the Lord every day. How? Read your Bible. Let God speak to you through what you read. Pray every day—ask God for wisdom. Let God grow you from the inside out! Most of all, keep focused on Jesus. You grow, He forgives, and you find peace.

"No discipline is enjoyable while it is happening – it is painful! But afterward there will be a peaceful harvest of right living for those who are trained in this way."
Hebrews 12:11 (New Living Translation)

#116 That's Embarrassing! Theme: Mistakes

Are you turning red?

When I was sixteen, my parents owned a lake resort. One day, while walking on the dock, some attractive girls in bathing suits caught my attention. I was so entranced, I walked off the end of the dock—fully clothed! There were about fifty people on the beach, all watching! I was so embarrassed! Forrest Gump said it: "Stupid is as stupid does."

How do you feel when you trip and fall? Hey, you are not perfect—you are forgiven. Yet, because of Jesus, you are perfect in God's eyes, no matter how you appear to others. When you hang with other Christians, you are in an atmosphere of unconditional love. God's love is demonstrated in Jesus Christ.

Here's Our Prescription:

Accept the love. Get over the embarrassment. Don't turn red. Turn to God, and remember to show His kind of acceptance to others.

"So, humble yourselves under God's strong hand, and in his own good time he will lift you up. You can throw the whole weight of your anxieties upon him, for you are his personal concern."
1 Peter 5:6-7 (Phillips Translation)

#117 Ministry Mistakes Theme: Mistakes

Did you make a mistake?

Shelly was excited about reading the Scripture in church. She was given a remote microphone to pin on her blouse. However, she forgot to turn it off when she went to the restroom. Do you know what a resounding toilet flush sounds like in church? Have you ever been embarrassed by a mistake?

Sooner or later, everybody messes up. Yes, it happens to Christians, too. What do *you* do when it happens to you?

Here's Our Prescription:

Strive for excellence, accept your humanity, and cut yourself some slack. Remember, the Scripture says you carry His message in a fragile clay pot. We are all breakable! Once in a while, you might even be a cracked pot. However, as a believer, the light of Christ shines—through the cracks. That is God's power! It is one of the many miracles of faith. So, learn to laugh at yourself, and love on others when they make mistakes.

"But we have this treasure in jars of clay to show that this all-surpassing power is from God and not from us."
2 Corinthians 4:7 (New International Version)

#118 Failure Isn't Forever Theme: Mistakes

Is it the end?

Shortly after Jane started teaching Sunday school, she realized she didn't have those gifts or skills. She resigned, and she felt like a failure. At some point in your life, you have failed, too. I have done it many times! Doesn't everyone?

Years ago, I read the classic book *Failing Forward* by John Maxwell. John says that failure is not the end—it's a stepping stone to success.

Here's Our Prescription:

Failure is not forever. Jane didn't make it as a Sunday school teacher. However, she did discover she had the gift of service. Now she serves in the church office—and loves it. Failing is something you do; it is never who you are. In Christ, you are always a winner. So, when you fail, and you will, fail forward! And don't look back!

"Let your eyes look directly forward, and your gaze be straight before you."
Proverbs 4:25 (Revised Standard Version)

#119 Whoops! Theme: Mistakes

Are you saying "whoops" often?

I love my son, Jon. However, as a young boy, he was challenged with absentminded adolescence. "Jon, did you take your vitamin?" "Whoops." "Jon, did you pick up your dirty clothes?" "Whoops." "Jon, did you remember to feed your dog?" "Whoops." Good news: He grew out of it, *almost* entirely! He likely inherited it from his dad.

You might think all the mistakes would end when you become an adult. But they don't, do they? Everyone makes mistakes. Yet, many can be prevented.

Here's Our Prescription:

God has given you parents, pastors, bosses, and leaders—people with more wisdom than you. Scripture says, "A wise person has many counselors." Whether you are at home, with your kids, in your marriage, at work, or in church, remember: Wise advice is great medicine. And, remember: "Whoops," you're forgiven!

"Become wise by walking with the wise; hang out with fools and watch your life fall to pieces."
Proverbs 13:20 (The Message)

#120 Dreaming Again Theme: Vision

Do you dare to dream?

You may not know what the future holds, but as a believer, you know Who holds the future! No matter how disrupted you feel today, God has a plan for your life. God will give you divine direction whenever you listen to Him. Would you like to know what the Ruler of the universe has in mind for you?

Here's Our Prescription:

Spend time with God. Speak to Him in prayer. Read His Word, the Bible. Grasp His vision of your destiny. Expect Him to speak to you. It may come as a notion, an idea, or a comment from a friend. Pray for guidance for all your choices, every decision. Watch for opportunities that come your way. Are they God-orchestrated? At first, it may not be clear. Yet, when you look back, perhaps years later, you will know: God was in it. He always is.

"...God has made everything beautiful for its own time. He has planted eternity in the human heart, but even so, people cannot see the whole scope of God's work from beginning to end."
Ecclesiastes 3:11 (New Living Translation)

#121 Decisions, Decisions! Theme: Vision

Do you hear all the noise?

Mike is perplexed. He's thinking about going to college. He also has a possible job offer. His girlfriend wants him to move back home. His car payments are constantly nagging. In a world with so many choices, how do *you* make decisions?

How do you discover God's direction?

Here's Our Prescription:

Get rid of the noise—the clutter in your life. Go to a quiet place—and listen for God. Spend a whole day or several days—whatever you can schedule. Get into the Bible. Allow the Lord to speak without the clutter. Learn about God's character: His passion, His priorities, what He wants for your life. Pray. Ask God for direction. In a quiet environment, God will direct your life. Lose the noise, and listen!

"...take on an entirely new way of life – a God-fashioned life, a life renewed from the inside and working itself into your conduct as God accurately reproduces his character in you."
Ephesians 4:23-24 (The Message)

#122 God Territory Theme: Vision

Do you ever find life overwhelming?

I asked Dale if he would like to go with me to El Salvador to help prepare for a conference. He looked at me like I was from another planet. He said, "I've never done that!"

Do you ever feel like you are stretched beyond your limit? Did you consider that you were just about to enter "God territory"? Anyone can do what comes naturally. However, you really experience God when it can only be done supernaturally. Your faith grows when you are literally not in control.

Here's Our Prescription:

Don't limit God. Before you say, "I've never done that," ask these questions: "Is God in it? Does God want it?" If you lived your life like that, do you think it would make a difference? It would! Try God; trust God. Step out into God's control.

"Don't drag your feet. Be like those who stay the course with committed faith and then get everything promised to them."
Hebrews 6:12 (The Message)

#123 Just for You Theme: Vision

Are you lost?

I was driving through the city and stopped for a light. The bumper sticker on the car in front of me said, "Don't follow me, I'm lost." Do you ever feel the need for God's direction? Do you wonder if God has a vision for the direction He wants you to go? Who He wants you to be? What He wants you to become?

God uniquely created you. He has a special calling just for you. It is His plan for your life.

Here's Our Prescription:

Don't limit God's direction to a crisis. Look for it every day. When you use your Bible, don't just read and pray. Spend time listening. Think: "What is He saying to me right now?" The Ruler of the universe has a special plan just for you. Ask God to help you find it! Don't be lost. Be found! On your journey, put God in the driver's seat.

> *"You created every part of me; you put me together in my mother's womb.... The days allotted to me had all been recorded in your book, before any of them ever began."*
>
> *Psalm 139:13, 16b (Good News Translation)*

#124 How Are You Wired? Theme: Vision

How are you wired?

Linda stared at her coffee cup and wondered. The following day, she would turn 30—a day she thought would never come. She considered the meaning of her life. Even as a Christian, she wasn't sure what God wanted for her life.

Have you ever experienced that kind of gut check? Guess what? Most of us have. All of us should—often. Don't ever settle for a job. Look for God's calling on your life. Anyone can achieve success. Strive for nothing less than significance.

Here's Our Prescription:

Read your Bible on a regular basis. Discover how God has uniquely wired you. Learn about your spiritual gifts. Focus on your strengths, what excites you, where you find meaning. Then structure your life according to those gifts, your uniqueness, and what ignites your passion. Where is God pulling you? You will discover meaning, God's plan for you. Never forget: You are divinely wired to be you!

"For he chose us in him before the creation of the world to be holy and blameless in his sight."
Ephesians 1:4 (New International Version)

#125 Hot Button   Theme: Vision

What is your hot button?

If you have heard me speak in a conference, you probably heard me introduced like this: "Kent says his reason for being born is to help Christians and churches become more effective in fulfilling the Great Commission." That is my *personal* mission statement. It is why I get up in the morning. It is my hot button. You might call it my passion. It is God's call on my life. What is yours?

My friend Wayne Hamit said that your passion is what makes you laugh and what makes you cry. God has put a unique passion in every person, including you! It reflects your calling. You are a unique part of His plan to impact the world! Find your passion, and you will discover your calling.

Here's Our Prescription:

Search for your divine hot button! What excites, and ignites, your passion? What could you live for? What would you die for? On your worst day, what excites you? Your calling, by your Creator, reveals why you were born.

"And don't be wishing you were someplace else or with someone else. Where you are right now is God's place for you. Live and obey and love and believe right there."
1 Corinthians 7:17a (The Message)

#126 God Is Calling Theme: Vision

Do you wish you had more energy?

Are you tired—worn out—even when you are serving God? Or working at your job? If so, remember this principle: It is not how much you work. More often, it is what you do.

For a few years, I had to focus on administrative work to get our ministry through a tough time. It drained me. Those close to me suggested I cut out some of my speaking engagements because I was tired. I said, "No! They energize me." Why? Teaching is one of my gifts. It is part of my calling. Administration is not. That explains part of my "divine profile"—from God. What is yours?

Here's Our Prescription:

Focus your work on areas that energize you. What has God called you to do? Focus on God's calling and your gifts. It is never about money, fame, or constant fun. It is about God's "sweet spot" for you. You will be energized!

"The world and all its wanting, wanting, wanting is on the way out—but whoever does what God wants is set for eternity."
1 John 2:17 (The Message)

#127 Fulfillment

Theme: Self-Esteem

Are you working?

Whether you are a stay-at-home mom or dad, a student in the classroom, or an executive at the office—it is called "work." Do you ever complain about work? Normally, productivity brings fulfillment. When you accomplish something, you impact others—some you may never meet. Work gives a healthy sense of pride.

Achievement fills a hole in your soul. You were created to be productive. And, you can be even more effective!

Here's Our Prescription:

Beyond work, you need "discretionary" time. Give ten percent of that time to serve God. Volunteer at your church. Serve your community. Help those who are helpless. Go beyond the profit motive. Add value to the lives of others—in the eternal dimension. Demonstrate God's love. The next time someone asks for help, don't look at it as more work. See it as an opportunity: the gift of fulfillment. You have a job, a role, and a ministry. God created you for all three—in balance.

"We do not live for ourselves only, and we do not die for ourselves only."
Romans 14:7 (Good News Translation)

#128 Your Self-Worth

Theme: Self-Esteem

So, what do you do?

A soda vendor once defined his title as "Assistant Chief Beverage Dispenser and Paper Product Specialist." Ever notice that some people put their worth in their title? How do you evaluate your self-esteem? Does it come from what you do or from who you are in Christ?

Here's Our Prescription:

Don't measure your worth simply by what you do. Your divine and eternal value is entirely based on God's love for you in Jesus Christ. All people are valued the same. You have unique gifts that direct what you do—but what you do doesn't define *who* you are. To know the difference makes all the difference. God the Father created you. Jesus died for you. The Holy Spirit has gifted you.

Celebrate who you are *in Christ* and rejoice in whatever He has led you to do. Use your platform of life to demonstrate your faith in God. Don't hide your faith—live it.

"Concentrate on doing your best for God, work you won't be ashamed of, laying out the truth plain and simple."
2 Timothy 2:15 (The Message)

#129 Pressure Cooker

Theme: Self-Esteem

Do you live for excellence?

Ever feel like you are under pressure to perform for God? Or, do you have the other challenge—apathy and lack of integrity in your service? We all need balance. How do you get it?

As a believer, strive for excellence. God deserves your very best. However, don't beat yourself up. The passion for excellence is not the assumption of perfection. In fact, the Bible says we are just the opposite!

Here's Our Prescription:

Remember, you are not a human *doing*. You are a human *being*. We are all weak and fragile. You, like the rest of us, may have even experienced a failure or two! Yet, God uses you in powerful ways—even though you are not perfect. So, set your goals high, and make your standards lofty. God deserves your very best. However, when you come up short, remember: God is merciful and forgiving. And, He is not done with you yet!

"There has never been the slightest doubt in my mind
that the God who started this great work in you
would keep at it and bring it to a flourishing finish on
the very day Christ Jesus appears."
Philippians 1:6 (The Message)

#130 Occupational Hazards Theme: Self-Esteem

How do you work?

Marcia's attitude about her job was incredibly negative. Her only motivation was a paycheck. She chronically complained and wasted time whenever possible. At the end of the day, she was the first one out the door. Are you like Marcia? Working for a living instead of living to work?

Here's Our Prescription:

Take inventory of your work life. Are you at the place God wants you to be? Did you ask God to direct you toward your occupation? Are you where He wants you? Get with God in prayer and ask for help to figure out what is right for you. Then, pray the same way about your unpaid service at church. Whatever you do, work as God has directed you. Your attitude will change from drudgery to adventure! When you serve where God intends, you don't have a job. You are on a mission from God.

"Whatever you do, work at it with all your heart, as though you were working for the Lord and not for people."
Colossians 3:23 (Good News Translation)

#131 Reaching Out

Theme: Self-Esteem

Can you help a guest?

Ever experience a lonely crowd? I remember the first time I flew alone to Germany. I went from the airport to the train station and had to figure out which train to get on. I was operating in a language I barely knew. I felt small, alone, and a little scared.

When our Church Doctor consultants help congregations, we attend the worship services—incognito. We become "undercover visitors." Some of our experiences are great. Many are horrible. I've even had a greeter hand me a bulletin and not even look at me! He was talking to a friend. In that crowd, I felt lonely. Often, those who visit a church feel the same way.

Here's Our Prescription:

Be a big brother or sister—in Christ. Become an "undercover greeter." Greet new people. Show them around. Introduce them to the staff and your friends. Sit with them. Invite them to fellowship. You could be the difference in whether they come back or not. Help them meet Jesus and discover the crowd is never lonely with Him.

"Be sure to give each other a warm greeting."
Romans 16:16a (Contemporary English Version)

#132 Spiritual Starvation

Theme: Self-Esteem

Are you getting enough to eat?

A woman bought a parrot, but it never talked. The store owner suggested buying a mirror. That didn't work. Then she got a ladder. The parrot still didn't talk. Then she added a swing. Nothing worked. Finally, the parrot died. The store owner said, "Did the bird say anything?" "Yes," the woman replied. "Right before he died, he asked, 'Don't they sell food at that pet store?'"

Are you a starving Christian? You might be spiritually anemic and not even realize it!

Here's Our Prescription:

Feed on the "spiritual food" God has given you in the Bible. When you are spiritually anemic, it can be easy to forget how much God loves you, how He guides your life, how much He helps you. You become fragile. You are truth-starved! Do you worry about our world? The Scripture feeds you on the inside. When you are right inside, your outside world gets more manageable.

"Anyone who lives on milk, being still an infant, is not acquainted with the teaching about righteousness. But solid food is for the mature, who by constant use have trained themselves to distinguish good from evil."

Hebrews 5:13-14 (New International Version)

#133 Hole in Your Heart

Theme: Self-Esteem

Are you feeling empty?

A man interviewing Billy Graham asked, "Why are you always so optimistic?" Dr. Graham replied, "I read the end of the Bible and discovered God won." Nothing fills your heart like your relationship with Jesus Christ.

We are all born with a hole in our hearts. This hole is not physical, but spiritual. Some people spend a lifetime trying to fill it with possessions, people—even sin. However, in the end, there is no lasting value.

Here's Our Prescription:

Remember, possessions and people come and go. Sin makes tempting promises, but never delivers. Self-esteem based on temporary achievements always disappoints. Your self-worth is healthy when it is based on your relationship with Jesus. He can fill the hole in your heart like nothing else. Invite him to fill that void today. You need more of Jesus. Count on this: He wants all of you!

"It's in Christ that we find out who we are and what we are living for. Long before we first heard of Christ and got our hopes up, he had his eye on us, had designs on us for glorious living, part of the overall purpose he is working out in everything and everyone."

Ephesians 1:11-12 (The Message)

#134 Influential Impact

Theme: Witnessing

Does your contact make impact?

Sam and Bob worked together for years. As they developed a relationship, Sam shared the difference Christ made in his life. He told Bob some of his "God stories." Over the following years, Bob's life turned around. He became a believer—and his eternal destiny became entirely different.

Immortality lies not in what you leave behind, but in the people your life has touched. You can influence others as much as God has influenced you.

Here's Our Prescription:

Think about your circle of relationships. Pray every day for God to "open doors" for sharing your faith. As a Christian, you have "God stories" about how God has worked in your life. If every Christian shared their stories, this world would significantly change—one person at a time. It can start with you!

"Be wise in the way you act with people who are not believers, making the most of every opportunity."
Colossians 4:5 (New Century Version)

#135 Storytelling

Theme: Witnessing

Does your life showcase faith?

Enthusiasm for God is contagious. You likely caught it from others. Has anyone caught it from you? Sometimes the idea of sharing faith feels scary. What makes you nervous? Offending someone? Rejection?

Sharing your faith with someone is actually simple. It is telling two stories.

Here's Our Prescription:

Start by telling your own story: how God has made a difference in your life. You don't need Bible passages or theological statements. Just tell it like it is. It is difficult for anyone to argue about your changed life. Then, tell the Christmas story. Tell how Jesus came and why. Tell what He did. You shouldn't preach. Don't rehearse or memorize the story. Simply be yourself. People hear a lot of stories. But this one can change them for eternity. It could become their story. What if they don't change? That is not on you. You can always tell another story. Big change is occasionally instant. Sometimes it takes time. It's a God thing. You are just the messenger.

"...we loved you so much, we were delighted to share with you not only the gospel of God but our lives as well."
1 Thessalonians 2:8 (New International Version)

#136 Flicker of Light

Theme: Witnessing

Are you feeling insignificant?

Late one night I was working in our barn. When I turned out the lights, it was so dark I couldn't see. I wished for a flashlight. Even the tiniest light would have made a big difference. I felt lost in my own barn! A tiny candle would have helped so much!

Do you ever consider yourself insignificant?

Here's Our Prescription:

Keep Jesus' words in mind. He identified Himself as the "light of the world." You can shine that light to others. There are people in your circle of relationships who are discouraged, frustrated, hopeless, and troubled. You may not be a floodlight, like some famous evangelist. Yet, your "flicker" can change the world, one life at a time. Your church is a cluster of tiny lights. Together, you change your community. It can begin with you. Turn to Jesus. He will turn on your light! Miracles will follow.

"You are the light of the world."
Matthew 5:14a (New International Version)

#137 Watch God Show Up! Theme: Witnessing

How do you share?

As we were eating dinner, the doorbell rang. A couple of strangers wanted to know if I was saved and knew Jesus. Well, I am, and I do. But I wondered what these strangers were doing interrupting my supper. Is Jesus one who would barge into your house?

Do experiences like that shut down your enthusiasm for sharing your faith? Don't worry! God's approach is not to "beat people over the head." His plan is to love them into His Kingdom.

Here's Our Prescription:

Develop your platform. Most people become believers when others share their faith in a genuine caring and sharing *relationship*. As you develop relationships, you are building a personal platform. When that base is strong, stand on it—and share your faith from your heart. Don't preach at people. Just tell your story. Share how God has made an incredible difference in your life. Build the relational platform, share what Jesus means to you, and watch God show up. If you are happy, and you know it, show your joy.

"'...I bring you the most joyful news ever announced, and it is for everyone!'"
Luke 2:10 (The Living Bible)

#138 Let Go, Let God

Theme: Witnessing

Are you scared?

Martha has been building a relationship with her new neighbor, Linda. Linda's life is a mess. She suffered terribly from an abusive relationship with a husband who is now gone. She has some health issues. Her car was totaled last week. Thankfully, she wasn't hurt. Yet, it got her thinking about life—and death. Linda needs hope. As a Christian, Martha wants to share her hope in Jesus. However, she is afraid. Are you?

Here's Our Prescription:

If you are afraid, maybe you put too much pressure on yourself. Sharing good news about Jesus is something God wants to do *through* you. Put yourself in God's hands. Trust Him. Let go. Let God change lives for eternity through you. Your mouth belongs to the God who made you! When you trust Him, you will be amazed at how easy it is.

"But Moses pleaded with the LORD, 'O Lord, I'm not very good with words. I never have been, and I'm not now, even though you have spoken to me. I get tongue-tied, and my words get tangled.' Then the Lord asked Moses, 'Who makes a person's mouth?'"
Exodus 4:10-11a (New Living Translation)

#139 Faith or Football?

Theme: Witnessing

What do you talk about?

The family gathered together at Uncle George's for a Christmas party. Bob thought it might be a good time to talk about Jesus—after all, it was His birthday. George snapped, "Look, Bob, in this family we don't talk about politics or religion." So, they discussed football.

Ever feel hesitant to talk about your faith? Some Christians believe it is inappropriate. Why? They are afraid to offend someone!

Here's Our Prescription:

If your friends or family don't believe in Jesus, and you really care about them—take the risk! Be sensitive. Sharing your faith makes a difference in life. It is not intruding, but telling the truth! Don't you think all heaven would rejoice if you simply told the truth? You can change the world, one person at a time! And God will impact others for eternity.

"'...we can't keep quiet about what we've seen and heard.'"
Acts 4:20 (The Message)

#140 Windows 3:16

Theme: Witnessing

Are you looking through windows of opportunity?

We went to visit Roger's son, Paul, in the hospital. On the door was a sign: "We have good news in this room. Ask us." Written underneath was John 3:16: "For God loved the world so much He gave His only son. Whoever believes in Him has eternal life." People who came to see Roger's son (including doctors, nurses, and housekeeping staff) quickly grasped the life-or-death dimensions of the situation. They also found people who embraced the good news about Jesus.

This is a true story. Paul lived, "against all odds." That sign on the door was a statement of faith. Paul—who the doctors expected to die—represented a miracle.

Here's Our Prescription:

Watch for people who are experiencing challenges—an illness or a tragedy. Look for those in transition—moving or changing jobs. In these times, they are more receptive to faith in Jesus Christ. It is your window of opportunity. Watch for divine windows. Be ready to share eternal hope.

"Always be prepared to give an answer to everyone who asks you to give the reason for the hope that you have."

1 Peter 3:15b (New International Version)

#141 Pro-portion   Theme: Financing

Show me the money!

As Pastor Jason began his sermon, Bob cringed. "Not another message about money!" However, Bob didn't understand. It wasn't a message about money. It was about giving. There is a world of difference! Do you struggle in the financial department of your spiritual life?

Here's Our Prescription:

The issue is never about money. It is about faith. It is understanding what God wants. Christians don't give as they are able. They give because they believe. God challenges us to return a percentage. It is called "proportionate giving." As God blesses you, you give more back. God allows you to "exercise" your faith. You can't outgive God. Why? When you are generous with God, He is even more generous with you. Don't try to figure it out. It is a miracle!

"Remember this: Whoever sows sparingly will also reap sparingly, and whoever sows generously will also reap generously."
2 Corinthians 9:6 (New International Version)

#142 Pick Your Pockets Theme: Financing

Have you made money?

Someone said, "Why snatch at wealth, hoard it, and stock it? Your casket, you know, will not have a pocket!" You can't take it with you. Have you ever seen a U-Haul behind a hearse?

Wealth comes in two forms. Left pocket wealth is your paycheck. As a Christian, you give a portion of that back to God. Right pocket wealth is accumulated wealth, like real estate you sell that has appreciated. It could be money you have inherited. It represents your opportunity to invest in the big picture of what God is doing. A friend of mine just sold his company. He wanted me to know that a check is coming for Church Doctor Ministries to help more churches to grow. He said, "I'm excited! It is all God's anyway." He is right: All resources belong to God. He has given us the privilege of generosity.

Here's Our Prescription:

Check both of your pockets! You simply can't outgive God. Can you believe it?

"And God can give more blessings than you need.
Then you will always have plenty of everything –
enough to give to every good work."
2 Corinthians 9:8 (New Century Version)

#143 Not To, but From — Theme: Financing

What is your view?

Have you heard this? "A person who *earns* is industrious. One who *spends* is well furnished. One who *saves* is prepared. And one who *gives* is blessed." So, how do you give? Do you give *to* your church, the budget, specific programs, or missions? Or, do you give *from* the abundance of God's blessings?

You should make the most of what God gives. It is all God's gift to you! God deals out joy in the present, the *now*. When you support God's work, you give *back* to God. You are not giving to a program. You're not financing "the church" to keep it afloat. You respond with thanksgiving to God for His generosity.

Here's Our Prescription:

Return a portion of God's blessings to His work. It is never a financial transaction. It is an act of faith. Since you can't outgive God, you can practice "hilarious generosity." Ministry is never short on money—just people short on faith. "What's in your wallet?" Even more, "Who's in your heart?"

"Yes, we should make the most of what God gives,
both the bounty and the capacity to enjoy it, accepting
what's given and delighting in the work."
Ecclesiastes 5:19 (The Message)

#144 Big Picture Theme: Financing

Are you going beyond?

Winston Churchill said, "We make a living by what we get, but we make a life by what we give." Ministries are often paralyzed by a lack of finances. With all the potential resources, God's work should never be financially crippled. The Bible says you can't outgive God. Mathematically, it doesn't compute. Generous giving is a spiritual miracle. God is the Master of abundance, not the slave of scarcity. He says you should test Him, and let Him prove it!

Here's Our Prescription:

Set aside ten percent of your income for your own congregation. Then, find "big-picture" ministries that impact beyond your church. Set aside at least five percent for those who serve beyond the church—impacting the world beyond you. It is not a sacrifice. It is an investment. And, God *will* bless you. Let Him prove it!

"This most generous God…is more than extravagant with you. He gives you something you can then give away, which grows into full-formed lives, robust in God, wealthy in every way, so that you can be generous in every way, producing with us great praise to God."
2 Corinthians 9:10-11 (The Message)

#145 S-t-r-e-t-c-h Theme: Financing

Can you stretch?

Billy Graham said, "If a person gets his attitude toward money straightened out, then almost all areas of his life will be straightened out." When it comes to supporting God's work, are you generous? Or, do you give God the leftovers—what you didn't really need?

Here's Our Prescription:

Stretch yourself. What if everyone in your church gave an additional three percent? Your congregation could start additional ministries and touch more lives, with greater impact on your community. Let it start with you. Stretch your faith. If no one ever took risks, Michelangelo would have painted the Sistine Chapel floor, not the ceiling. Move out on the spiritual limb. That is where you find the fruit. Make a difference. Let God stretch your generosity!

"All the believers were together and shared everything. They would sell their land and the things they owned and then divide the money and give it to anyone who needed it."
Acts 2:44-45 (New Century Version)

#146 Leap! Theme: Financing

How do you feel about money?

A boy had a dollar and a quarter for the Sunday offering. When the plate came around, he put in the quarter, but kept the dollar. Afterward, his father asked why he kept the dollar. The boy replied, "The pastor said, 'God loves a cheerful giver,' so I stayed happy by keeping the dollar!'" Can you relate to that little boy? Are you missing the joy of extravagant generosity?

Here's Our Prescription:

Take the leap of faith. Risk, and see if God doesn't supernaturally pour out blessings like He promises. God says you should test Him, and He will bless you with abundance. When you are generous for His work, God is generous with you. It is said, "You can count the number of seeds in an apple, but you can't count the number of apples in a seed." You can't outgive God. Try it, and experience abundance.

"Put me to the test and you will see that I will open the windows of heaven and pour out on you in abundance all kinds of good things."
Malachi 3:10b (Good News Translation)

#147 One Percent — Theme: Financing

What is a percent?

I visited a church. They passed around the offering, as usual. After the pastor looked at it, he passed it around again! Money does play an important part in ministry. I read this years ago: "Did you know that, collectively, Christians in the world have thirteen billion dollars? Ninety percent of that is in the United States." Today, it is probably more. No matter what your financial status, think about this: God has generously invested in you, so you can invest in His work.

Here's Our Prescription:

The Bible calls it tithing—giving back ten percent. In faith, raise your giving by one percent for a year. As you do, thank God for investing in your life. Show your gratitude, and multiply His work! Your extra percent will impact people for eternity. After that year, ask yourself: Did you miss it? Then raise it one percent the next year. You see, financing God's work isn't about money. It is about ministry. It's an act of faith. You can't outgive God! So, multiply your impact—one percent at a time.

"The purpose of tithing is to teach you always to put God first in your lives."
Deuteronomy 14:23c (The Living Bible)

#148 Rat Race

Theme: Personal Growth

Are you in a hurry?

Someone said, "Even if you win the rat race, you're still a rat." Do you think time is your greatest enemy? Every day you get twenty-four hours, like everyone else.

How do you find time—to spend time—with God every day?

Here's Our Prescription:

Make time with Jesus a priority. Schedule it. Get out of the rat race. Get alone with God. Evaluate everything that requires your time. How will you invest in what really makes a difference in the long run? Perhaps you feel like you are a spiritual version of the Energizer Bunny. However, all Christians need their spiritual batteries recharged. Every day, schedule personal time with God: in prayer, in the Bible. Don't race through your prayers or reading of Scripture. Stop and *contemplate*. Listen for God's whisper in your ears and on your heart. That is how you win the big race—the marathon of life. Take it one day at a time, with God.

"...continue to grow in the grace and knowledge of our Lord and Savior Jesus Christ."
2 Peter 3:18a (Good News Translation)

#149 Accountability

Theme: Personal Growth

Are you trying to go at it alone?

John has been a Christian for thirty-seven years. He has a college education, a good job, and a great family. He goes to a wonderful church. But there is one area of life where he has been consistently unsuccessful. Though he has tried, John has never been able to develop a daily personal time with God. He wants to. He just doesn't know how. John is missing a greater part of life than he realizes. Does that describe you?

Here's Our Prescription:

Find a spiritual accountability partner. Ask someone you already know and like. Look for a Christian who has conquered the discipline to take time with God. Commit to one another. Help each other grow. Challenge each other to set aside some personal time with God—every day. Ask your partner to pray for you—and hold you accountable. It changed John's life. It can change yours. You will become more spiritually healthy.

"Take time and trouble to keep yourself spiritually fit."
1 Timothy 4:7b (Phillips Translation)

#150 Growth in Groups

**Theme:
Personal Growth**

Do you get together with others to learn from Scripture?

The African proverb says, "The Bible is so shallow a child can wade and so deep an elephant must swim." Learning about God and His great plan for your life is an amazing experience! While it is great to grow by yourself, Bible study alone should not be your only approach. There is strength—and wisdom—in numbers.

Here's Our Prescription:

Get into a group Bible study. Join a Sunday school class or a small group that meets in a home, at a restaurant, or at a park—anywhere. Group dynamics are different than when you study or read the Bible by yourself. Why? You learn from each other. You grow, as God uses the insights of others. And, they learn from you. You demonstrate your commitment to God and to one another. The group provides accountability. If you don't show up, you will be missed. Through the group experience, everyone benefits. Your life will overflow with the wealth of God's wisdom. Take the plunge. Join a Bible study group. Jump into the depth of God's Word. You will learn from God *and* each other.

"...you yourselves are full of goodness, filled with knowledge and competent to instruct one another."
Romans 15:14 (New International Version)

#151 Quiet!

Theme: Personal Growth

Do you own earplugs?

The first church I pastored was in the inner city of Detroit. I loved that congregation. But I grew weary of the noise of the city. Day and night, there seemed to be noise everywhere: cars, trucks, and sirens. We all need time alone with God and without distractions.

Do you have a quiet time when you read the Bible and pray, but also spend time meditating on what God is saying? For that, you need a quiet place.

Here's Our Prescription:

Find a place that works for you. Jim is a businessman who spends his lunch hour in a corner of the warehouse. Mary is a quiet, stay-at-home mom who settles down with God after the kids get on the bus. Jon and Andrew are hunters who love to be alone with God in a deer stand. Vi is a woman who meets with God in her garden. Find your place, your time, with your God! And be quiet!

"Very early the next morning before daylight, Jesus got up and went to a place where he could be alone and pray."
Mark 1:35 (Contemporary English Version)

#152 Take Inventory!

Theme: Personal Growth

Are you keeping track?

When we consult churches, one of the questions we ask the people is whether or not they have grown spiritually in the last year. Some say they have. Many say they are about the same. Quite a few say they have declined in their spiritual growth. What if we analyzed your church and it showed that more than fifty percent of the people said their spiritual health was stagnant? Would you be one of them? I challenge you today: Perform a personal, spiritual "gut check."

Here's Our Prescription:

Take inventory. Have you grown spiritually in the last year? Take a serious, prayerful look in your spiritual mirror. Do it regularly, as a life habit. What priorities do you need to change? What attitudes are stunting your spiritual growth? Pray, and ask God for help. Do it today. And tomorrow. And the next day. And the day after. God will help. You will grow. And a year from now, when you look into your spiritual mirror, more likely, you won't just see yourself. You will see more clearly that God is with you. You will recognize that you have grown spiritually—closer to God.

"Let us examine our ways and turn back to the LORD."
Lamentations 3:40 (Good News Translation)

#153 Bookworm

**Theme:
Personal Growth**

Do you like to learn?

Henry Ford said, "Anyone who stops learning is old, whether they're twenty or eighty." Are you ready for an evaluation? Make an analysis of how much time you spend reading in a given week. Most people read every day: newspapers, sports magazines, novels, texts, emails, Instagram posts, websites, etc. You might be amazed about how much time you spend.

Here's Our Prescription:

Try this experiment for a month: Carve out twenty percent of your reading time for Christian material. Dedicate ten percent for personal Christian improvement of your faith and life. Spend the other ten percent for how you can contribute to the benefit and productivity of your church. Go online and check out all the Christian books. There are many resources to help you. Learn and grow as a Christian. Give twenty percent of your growth time for spiritual advancement. Invest in the best—in what matters most!

"Commit yourself to instruction; listen carefully to words of knowledge."
Proverbs 23:12 (New Living Translation)

#154 Ears to Hear

Theme: Personal Growth

Are you listening?

Ever notice that God has created us with only one mouth but two ears? There is a message there! You listen a lot. By listening to the right content, you will move forward in your spiritual growth.

Here's Our Prescription:

Try this experiment: Carve out twenty percent of your "listening time" for spiritual growth. Use half that time for your personal growth. Take the other ten percent for growth as a responsible member of your church. Listen to a Christian radio station in your car. Focus on Christian teaching. Learn how you can help your church become more effective in outreach. There are many audio resources to choose from. Ask God to direct you in your personal growth and for the effectiveness of your church. Don't allow your listening to become passive—"in one ear and out the other." Receive it in both ears, take it to heart, and contribute to your spiritual growth.

"Get all the advice and instruction you can, so you will be wise the rest of your life."
Proverbs 19:20 (New Living Translation)

#155 TNT Theme: Comfort

Is your Christian life explosive?

Remember those cartoons where the characters are blown up with TNT? After the smoke clears, they are dazed and covered with ashes. It is comical. Many Christians have also been hit with a different brand of TNT. I call it *tension* and *turmoil.* They are two ingredients that blow Christian relationships to pieces. There is nothing funny about it. And, your life at church is not immune to TNT! Tension and turmoil can *throw* you, or it can *grow* you.

Here's Our Prescription:

Instead of focusing on the negatives, focus on the positives. Designate times during the day to pray specifically for tensions in your life. Right now, list the tensions you face and the real source of the turmoil. Then draw the cross of Jesus on top of them. Tension and turmoil are never fun. However, remember what the Apostle Paul said, "God works for the good of those who love him." These challenges don't seem like growth opportunities at the time. Yet, looking back, you will recognize: God was at work, growing you.

"'... I will build my church, and all the powers of hell will not conquer it.'"
Matthew 16:18b (New Living Translation)

#156 Divine Math   Theme: Comfort

Is there trouble brewing in your church?

Some mathematical principles apply to Christians like you and me. Jesus told His disciples to multiply believers in His name. God then added to their number daily. You could also say we are all equal in the sight of the Lord. Yet, whoever taught Christians to divide?

Church splits are painful. I met a couple who vowed they would never join another church. If that has happened to you, if your church is in danger of splitting, or if you have serious tensions with another Christian—there is hope.

Here's Our Prescription:

Christians aren't perfect, but Jesus is. He loves those who follow Him. He gave His life for them. He loves His church. He is the Head of it. He gave His life for you. And, He loves you. Draw closer to Jesus. He is aware of your challenges. Let Him add to your strength and multiply your joy. His love cancels division, and that equals harmony! Harmony brings us together as a team. That allows God to grow His Kingdom, through us, exponentially. You can count on it!

"Above all, love each other deeply, because love covers over a multitude of sins."
1 Peter 4:8 (New International Version)

#157 Boat Rocking Theme: Comfort

Are you rocking the boat?

Nothing stirs up Christians like the prospect of change. Yet, the secular world acts like it loves change. Some believers seem to be allergic to it. If someone proposes change at church, do you run away? Do you cause waves that rock the spiritual boat?

Perhaps you are looking for a leisurely sail. What if it is God who is allowing waves in your life? It is only a boat moving forward that makes waves. You could say that Jesus is the biggest boat-rocker who ever lived. He challenged people, traditions, and the status quo. He stretched people so they would grow. He was such a boat-rocker, a group of Pharisees and scribes had him killed. However, He rocked the world with a resurrection! Then He sent His followers to rock the world for eternity.

Here's Our Prescription:

If your boat is rocking, have no fear. Perhaps Jesus is moving you forward. Stand firm on Jesus. Let God change you—and grow you. Allow God to use you, and your church, to move our world toward Him.

"...the one who stands firm to the end will be saved."
Matthew 24:13 (New International Version)

#158 Dive In! Theme: Comfort

Are you testing the water?

Ever notice how people at the swimming pool put their toes into the water? If it's too cold, they won't get in. On the assessment of a few toes, some pass up the whole pool!

Are you dipping your toes into God's work? Do you back away or sit out because it feels uncomfortable? Do you miss the joy of serving the King of the universe because ministry comes disguised as hard work? Imagine being a Christian in Korea today. There, they "throw" Christians into serving! With little training, Korean Christians are often in the thick of ministry before they can even think about their comfort. Consider the disciples in a boat on the water in a storm—and Jesus is sleeping!

Here's Our Prescription:

Dive into God's work! Splash past your comfort zone. God is more interested in your commitment than your comfort. He wants you to grow, serve, and enjoy His adventure. Take a leap of faith!

"Lord, when doubts fill my mind, when my heart is in turmoil, quiet me and give me renewed hope and cheer."

Psalm 94:19 (The Living Bible)

#159 JOY **Theme: Comfort**

Can you spell?

You can spell the word "joy." However, did you know the letters represent the recipe for a *life* of joy? "J" stands for Jesus. Jesus wants to come first in your life. "O" stands for others. The Apostle Paul says, "Consider others more important than yourself." "Y" stands for you. True joy puts Jesus and others ahead of yourself.

During His life, Jesus put His Father—and others—first. For the JOY that was before him, Jesus endured the cross. He gave His life for you. By giving you life, His joy became complete.

Here's Our Prescription:

Write JOY on a card. Put it in your pocket or purse, in your car or on your bathroom mirror. Watch God make a difference in you. By putting Jesus and others ahead of yourself, God will make your joy complete. And next Christmas? If you sing "JOY to the World," it will be more meaningful than ever!

"Let us keep our eyes fixed on Jesus, on whom our faith depends from beginning to end. He did not give up because of the cross! On the contrary, because of the joy that was waiting for him, he thought nothing of the disgrace of dying on the cross...."
Hebrews 12:2 (Good News Translation)

#160 Heat Index Theme: Comfort

Are you sweating?

The pastor began worship on a hot summer morning: "We come before God with great humidity—I mean humility!" My friend Mick led a church in England. He called an engaging church "white-hot worship." In a weather forecast, the heat index tells how hot it *feels*, not how hot it actually is.

You have a heat index. It is measured by how close you are to God. If God directs you to where He is working, you are going to be hot! Hot is good! God wants you to be "on fire" for Him. That means moving out of the frigid religiosity of the frozen chosen: Christianity lite, business as usual. Want to spiritually sweat?

Here's Our Prescription:

Watch for God at work in your life. When you see Him in action, let go! Let God! Before you know it, you'll be on fire for God! Get close to God, and heat up your mission.

> *"I'm baptizing you here in the river, turning your old life in for a kingdom life. The real action comes next: The main character in this drama – compared to him I'm a mere stagehand – will ignite the kingdom life within you, a fire within you, the Holy Spirit within you, changing you from the inside out."*
> *Matthew 3:11 (The Message)*

#161 Petrified! Theme: Comfort

Are you feeling faint?

The pastor spoke to Don just before the fellowship meal. He said, "Don, why don't you lead the prayer tonight?" Don was petrified. All he could say was, "You do it this time, pastor. I'll do it next time." It could happen when you are asked to pray or have an opportunity to witness. Call it "spiritual deep freeze." Has it happened to you?

You want God-inspired courage. David had it. The Apostle Paul showed it. Peter had it, on and off—especially at the time of Jesus' crucifixion. Believers trust God as their source of strength.

Here's Our Prescription:

Let God take over! Pray for God's power, then get out of the way. Let go; let God. Do it right now. Pray this: "Lord, give me divine courage." Pray it daily. And watch God give you special courage in your life. Live life with God. You will do life with divine power!

"Be strong and of good courage; for you shall cause this people to inherit the land which I swore to their fathers to give them. Only be strong and very courageous...."
Joshua 1:6-7 (Revised Standard Version)

#162 Circle Up! Theme: Influence

Who is in your circle?

Leadership is influence. You may not realize it, but you influence many others—by what you do and with everything you say. You impact those in your circle of relationships: friends, relatives, neighbors, people at work or school. They are on your cell phone. They represent your primary circle of influence. Those who are unbelievers are your personal mission field. You are their missionary. Do you pray for them?

Would you like to be an effective influencer—for God?

Here's Our Prescription:

Identify those in your circle of relationships. Think about your Christian values. How do they come through in what you say and do? Don't underestimate yourself—you are a person of influence. If you are alive in Christ, you are a "winner." God wants you to win people to Him. If they follow Jesus, they grow the circle of influence—God's winner's circle. Pray for those who don't know Jesus. Share what God has done in your life. Let Christ win them over through your influence. Be a winner!

"'But you are my witnesses.' God's Decree. 'You're my handpicked servant….'"
Isaiah 43:10 (The Message)

#163 Can You Relate? Theme: Influence

How do you relate?

Kathryn doesn't hold an office in the church. She is not the head of a committee or board. However, she is well respected and always talking with, well, just about everyone. Kathryn is a Christian "leader" – with no title or position. Why? She influences everyone she meets.

You, too, have influence – whether you know it or not.

Here's Our Prescription:

Think about those you know. You talk to them. You send texts. You email. As you interact, you influence them – in some way. Can you focus on being spiritually positive? Pray for God's help. Make sure you are in line with God's intentions before you speak. Start each day asking God to use you to influence those you know, so that – through you – they might come to know the Lord and grow in faith. Can you *relate* to that? Simply relate your faith in your relationships.

"…we always speak as God wants us to, because he has judged us worthy to be entrusted with the Good News. We do not try to please people, but to please God, who tests our motives."
1 Thessalonians 2:4 (Good News Translation)

#164 R-E-S-P-E-C-T Theme: Influence

Are you respected?

Think about those in your sphere of influence. They include friends, relatives, neighbors, those at work or school—and those at church. Now, think about which of them you really respect. What do they have in common? Here is my guess: They reflect high integrity. They look out for the needs of others. When our extended family meets for holidays, guess which ones I like and respect most? Those who ask me, "How is it going?" and actually wait to hear my reply. How do I know they care? Because they ask.

The Bible says we should watch for the concerns of others, not just our own. An old Chinese proverb says, "People all wrapped up in themselves make small packages." Those who look out for the needs of others have a lifestyle like Jesus.

Here's Our Prescription:

Ask God for a genuine interest in others. It will show when you ask, "How are you doing?" You will become a respected influencer. They will not only see you; they will see Jesus in you. They will not just hear you; they will hear Christ speaking through you. He will influence them eternally, using you!

"Don't look out only for your own interests, but take an interest in others, too."
Philippians 2:4 (New Living Translation)

#165 Authority — Theme: Influence

Give them a break!

Ever hear a friend at church tear down your pastor, complain about the church board, or make a sarcastic remark about your mayor or the leader of the country? When I was a kid, we played "follow the leader." It is similar to the concept "respect for authority." It is God's plan for the way the world should operate. It is nonnegotiable for Christians! What is your attitude toward those in authority? Your boss? The police? The politicians? Your church leaders? "Civility" is a word that means respect. Respect reflects that you are *civilized.*

Here's Our Prescription:

You don't have to agree with everything leaders say or do. You are expected to respect authority. Pray for those who lead. If they have issues or challenges, work toward helping them. If everyone did that, the world—and the way it works—would be influenced by your faith. Give them a break. Show respect. Whether they know it or not, leaders work for God.

"No one rules unless God has given him the power to rule, and no one rules now without that power from God.... The ruler is God's servant to help you."
Romans 13:1b,4a (New Century Version)

#166 Be a Plus! Theme: Influence

Do you invest in others?

It seems like every time I see John, I feel better after we talk. But almost every time I connect with Sylvia, I feel drained. Why is that?

When people see you, how do they react? Positively or negatively? Everyone you touch is influenced, for good or bad, by what you say and do. It reflects who you are. Are you a plus or a minus for those you encounter? How do you think people felt after they met Jesus? How do *you* feel around those who always have a negative comment or complaint?

Here's Our Prescription:

Influence others on behalf of the God you worship. Every day you impact people—positively or negatively. Your influence lifts them up or knocks them down. You are either a plus or minus to everyone you touch. Hang around those who influence for good—and let it rub off to others around you. Call it a plus movement. The influence of Jesus changes everything!

"...the people were astonished at seeing dumb men speak, crippled men healed, lame men walking about and blind men having recovered their sight. And they praised the God of Israel."
Matthew 15:31 (Phillips Translation)

#167 Winfluence — Theme: Influence

Do you share your faith?

Francis of Assisi said, "Preach the Gospel every day; if necessary, use words." If I asked you to share your faith, would you be nervous? Think about witnessing through influence. Call it *winfluence*! Think about what you do and say. How do you react to challenges? Do others see your faith in action when you face struggles?

Here's Our Prescription:

Let your faith shine. Who you are and what you do are as important as what you say. Be the message, and watch God give you opportunities to influence others for Christ. That is the power of winfluence!

Reflect on your actions the last twenty-four hours. Did they send the message you want? Determine that the next twenty-four hours, with God's help, will be better for those you influence. Repeat that during the next thirty days. Don't overlook *why* you influence. Point to Jesus.

"And whatever you do, whether in word or deed, do it all in the name of the Lord Jesus, giving thanks to God the Father through him."
Colossians 3:17 (New International Version)

#168 Empowerment Theme: Influence

Are you part of the solution?

Mary's husband is an alcoholic. It is a major challenge. Unfortunately, Mary is part of the problem. She looks the other way. She allows him to continue a habit that is killing him. She's an "enabler."

You choose how you impact others. You either help them rely on you or empower them to overcome, with God's help. Do you know someone with a serious difficulty? Do you want to do something positive and powerful to help?

Here's Our Prescription:

Follow Jesus' model to empower others. Focus on helping them reach a level where they operate *without* you. Help them get help—whatever it takes. Help them to experience their own victory. They may become stronger than you. Jesus' approach is to multiply yourself: to make an impact, not just an impression. Guide others to the level of restoration. This approach works. It is biblical. Let God use you to be part of the solution.

"It's true that moral guidance and counsel need to be given, but the way you say it and to whom you say it are as important as what you say."
1 Timothy 1:8 (The Message)

#169 You're Unique!

Theme:
Spiritual Gifts

Are you an original?

Have you ever thought about how unique you are? No one who has ever lived is exactly like you. You are an amazing example of God's infinite creativity! The Holy Spirit has given you spiritual gifts—supernatural attributes. When God created you, He broke the mold! When you became a Christian, you received a unique cluster of gifts.

Here's Our Prescription:

Read about spiritual gifts. Attend a workshop. Take a spiritual gifts reflection survey. You will discover the supernatural attributes God has given to you personally. You will begin to sense your uniqueness. Discovering your gifts is one of the most exciting experiences of your spiritual life. You will learn how and where God wants to use you. You are unique in all the world. When you discover your gifts, you will identify your unique purpose—*why* God made you! You will experience divine fulfillment—God's plan for your life! You will more effectively serve your church and God's mission.

"He did this to prepare all God's people for the work of Christian service, in order to build up the body of Christ."
Ephesians 4:12 (Good News Translation)

#170 They're Different!

Theme: Spiritual Gifts

Do you ever feel jealous?

It is amazing to watch Dorothy. She is at the top of her game when she washes dishes. Honestly, she loves serving food at church events. You can see it in her face—total enjoyment and satisfaction! I can't even relate. As for me? I hate washing dishes.

Why are people so different? Do you ever feel jealous because others can do some things better than you can?

Here's Our Prescription:

God has given you some unique gifts. Every believer has a gift mix. It is God's divine design. That doesn't make them better than you. It doesn't make you more gifted, either. It makes us all wonderfully different—unique! The Christian movement needs all the gifts to do God's work. So, discover and learn about your gifts. Find your sweet spot. See how God has made you. Find your niche. Don't feel jealous—get busy!

"A spiritual gift is given to each of us so we can help each other."
1 Corinthians 12:7 (New Living Translation)

#171 Your Divine Design

Theme: Spiritual Gifts

Do you know who you are?

Terry is one of the most miserable people I have ever met. He mopes around and complains all the time. He is basically unhappy with himself. What about you? Are you content with who you are? Are you comfortable in your own skin? Your uniqueness is God's gift to you. How you use it is your gift to God.

If you are frustrated about who you are, your challenge isn't about how God made you. God doesn't make mistakes! Perhaps the issue is that you haven't found your spot—your niche, your divine design.

Here's Our Prescription:

Discover *where* you belong. Where is your passion? What makes you laugh? What causes you to cry? When do you feel fulfilled? What really excites you? Find God's plan for you. Focus where you are most effective. Discover where you are productive. Identify where you experience fulfillment. Ask God to help you in your journey. You are uniquely wired by the Creator of the universe. You are gifted for personal growth. You are empowered by your Maker to impact this world. You are God's divine design.

"Now concerning spiritual gifts…I do not want you to be ignorant."
1 Corinthians 12:1 (New King James Version)

#172 The Niche

Theme: Spiritual Gifts

Where do you fit?

When I was a kid, I tried to play baseball. I would go down to the park and try to get in a game. The leader would gather the kids and take turns choosing players. I was the last one, after everyone else was picked. It became clear: In baseball, there wasn't a place for me. Do you ever feel like that? Then focus on what really counts!

Here's Our Prescription:

Cheer up! God has a place for everyone—including you! Don't ever forget: When others leave you out, God doesn't! On God's team, called church, there is a place for everyone. God's work needs your unique contribution. There is a special niche just for you. Look for it! Don't give up until you find it. If you are breathing, God has a place on His team for you! He will never leave you out. You can count on it: You've got a place in the greatest, most important movement in history! God uses people like you to change the eternal destiny of others.

"But our bodies have many parts, and God has put each part just where he wants it.... All of you together are Christ's body, and each of you a part of it."
1 Corinthians 12:18, 27 (New Living Translation)

#173 Your Divine Destiny

Theme: Spiritual Gifts

Where are you going?

When our daughter was in college, her first major was youth ministry. Then she thought about psychology. After that, it was elementary education. I said, "Only God knows what Laura will do!" That was my most intelligent comment! By God's design, she found her place in special education. She is amazing. Meanwhile, our son studied criminal justice in college, got a degree, and learned, more than anything else: Criminal justice is not for him! Today, he pastors a church! He found his niche.

We live in a complex world. The Apostle Paul began as an antagonist! Do you struggle with God's plan for you?

Here's Our Prescription:

Pray to God and listen! Stay in God's Word. Let Him speak to you. Experiment with different roles. Learn as much about yourself as you can. Get a handle on your strengths and weaknesses. Learn about your spiritual gifts. Keep your interest high and your anxiety low. Trust God. When the time is right, you will discover your divine destiny.

"Put God in charge of your work.... God made everything with a place and purpose.... It pays to take life seriously; things work out when you trust in God."
Proverbs 16:3a, 4a, 20 (The Message)

#174 The Dressing Room

Theme: Spiritual Gifts

Are you trying it on?

If you have looked for new clothes, you probably used a dressing room. There, you discovered whether or not the clothes fit. If they didn't, you kept searching. You didn't quit until you found the fit. Your spiritual journey has a dressing room, too. It is where you discover your unique spiritual gifts. It's how you find your *divine* fit. Spiritual gifts are supernatural abilities. They empower you to serve God most effectively. Every believer has gifts. It takes time and effort to discover them.

Here's Our Prescription:

Take a spiritual gifts discovery survey. Study the gifts that apply to you. Then, "try on" your gifts. Experiment in different areas of ministry. Ask, "What has God created me to do well? Where am I effective? Where do I sense fulfillment?" When you discover your "fit," you will serve Him with greater enthusiasm!

> *"For as in one body we have many members, and all the members do not have the same function, so we, though many, are one body in Christ, and individually members one of another. Having gifts that differ according to the grace given to us, let us use them…."*
>
> *Romans 12:4-6 (Revised Standard Version)*

#175 Like Mike?

Theme: Spiritual Gifts

Who are you?

Years ago, there was a song, "I wanna be like Mike." It was when kids across America wanted to be like basketball superstar Michael Jordan. Ever wish you had someone else's ability?

The Bible says there are different kinds of gifts, but the same Spirit. What if everyone had the same spiritual gifts? If everyone had the gift of teaching, there wouldn't be any students! If all Christians had the gift of leadership, there wouldn't be anyone to follow!

Here's Our Prescription:

If your church has a discovery approach about spiritual gifts, sign up! Read Romans 12, 1 Corinthians 12, and Ephesians 4. Take a survey to discover your gifts. Learn about your unique gift mix. Experience the joy of discovering your unique God-given gifts. You don't want to "be like Mike" or anyone else. Discover the person God uniquely made you to be. You will be content, fulfilled, and productive. There are no "volunteers" in the body of Christ, only those who have gifts given by the Holy Spirit.

"It is the one and only Spirit who distributes all these gifts. He alone decides which gift each person should have."
1 Corinthians 12:11 (New Living Translation)

#176 Window

Theme: Worldview

What do you see?

How do you look at the world? Can you know what God knows? In the Lord's Prayer, when you pray, "Your will be done," do you wonder, "How does that work?" Perhaps you have heard the story of the elephant. His leg was chained to a stake for so long, when they took it off, he never moved. In his mind, he was still chained. Are you chained by a lack of Bible knowledge? Are you missing God's will, what God wants for you?

Here's Our Prescription:

Think about how you understand this world. Read the Bible in a modern translation. Can you believe—and put into action—what God teaches? When you do, you will have a "biblical worldview." You will see the world the way God sees it: on issues like comfort, sex, authority, money, relationships, work, and sacrifice. Look at your life and the world through the window of God's Word. It will focus the way you see this world. It will change your life and impact those around you. It will empower your church, more than you could ever imagine.

"'My thoughts are nothing like your thoughts,' says the LORD. 'And my ways are far beyond anything you could imagine.'"
Isaiah 55:8 (New Living Translation)

#177 Boot Camp

Theme: Worldview

Are you reading your Bible?

While Grandpa was asleep, the kids put limburger cheese on his moustache. When he woke up, he said, "This room smells like limburger cheese!" Then he went outside and said, "The whole world smells like limburger cheese!" How does your world smell? Examine your worldview—your perspective. Your behavior is a result of your *worldview*: how you see your world and the way you understand how the world works.

Here's Our Prescription:

Enroll in your own "Bible Boot Camp." Read and study Scripture. God's Word is powerful, as relevant as today's news—and more reliable! Use a translation that speaks to you. The Bible has the power to change the way you see the world! When Scripture drives your behavior, you impact the world.

> *"There's nothing like the written Word of God for showing you the way to salvation through faith in Christ Jesus. Every part of Scripture is God-breathed and useful one way or another – showing us truth, exposing our rebellion, correcting our mistakes, training us to live God's way. Through the Word we are put together and shaped up for the tasks God has for us."*
> *2 Timothy 3:15-17 (The Message)*

#178 WWJD? Theme: Worldview

What would *you* do?

Many years ago, there was a bracelet and bumper sticker that read: "WWJD?" It stood for: "What would Jesus do?" It was, and is, a worldview. What drives your decisions? What steers your behavior? Who determines your lifestyle?

Ever catch yourself looking through the lens "WDIW" – "What do I want"? What we want isn't always what God wants. What we desire isn't always best for us. So, how do you make decisions?

Here's Our Prescription:

Spend more time in Scripture. Focus on God's character. Learn what He wants and expects. Pray, with every decision, "not what I want, but what you want, Lord." "What would Jesus do?" That question is *always* relevant—and best.

"Yes, all the things I once thought were so important are gone from my life. Compared to the high privilege of knowing Christ Jesus as my Master, firsthand, everything I once thought I had going for me is insignificant – dog dung. I've dumped it all in the trash so that I could embrace Christ and be embraced by him."
Philippians 3:8-9a (The Message)

#179 YWBD

Theme: Worldview

How do you make decisions?

The congregation stood for the Lord's Prayer. Everybody prayed together, "Your will be done, on earth as it is in heaven." Following worship, the members gathered for a meeting—and argued about what *they* wanted.

Do you want what God wants—really? Are you a YWBD person? YWBD: Your will be done! There is no question: God wants you to come to know Him. There is no debate: He wants you to share the good news about Jesus. Ask yourself, is that passion driving your life? Are you focusing on God's will—what God wants? Do you think about that? Do you live with the passion to reach those who are without God? That is what God wants.

Here's Our Prescription:

You can make a difference—by living "Your will be done." Start today. YWBD: Say it, mean it, pray it, live it. "Lord, make Your decisions my decisions—and my decisions Your decisions." It will change your life!

"...Jesus said, 'I tell you the truth, the Son can do nothing alone. The Son does only what he sees the Father doing, because the Son does whatever the Father does."

John 5:19 (New Century Version)

#180 Comfort-Driven

Theme: Worldview

Are you comfortable?

The restaurant air conditioning was blowing right on us. We mentioned it to the waiter, and he reseated us. We live in a comfort-driven culture. Have a headache? Take an aspirin. Eat too much? Buy bigger clothes. Bothered by insects? Put on repellent. Got in a dispute? Hire a lawyer. Seats hard? Pad the chairs.

However, if you're driven only by comfort, will you pray for those without God? Reaching unbelievers requires change—and change is not comfortable. God is more interested in your character than your comfort. He is more passionate about your effective life than your affluent life. Do you subordinate comfort for God's work? Missionaries do! Athletes say, "No pain, no gain." Jesus knew pain. Does that give you discomfort?

Here's Our Prescription:

Pray for God to use you—whatever it takes. Expect discomfort. Accept rejection. Ask for patience. Pursue perseverance. Experience transformation.

"Do not conform yourselves to the standards of this world, but let God transform you inwardly by a complete change of your mind. Then you will be able to know the will of God – what is good and is pleasing to him and is perfect."
Romans 12:2 (Good News Translation)

#181 Reflection

Theme: Worldview

Do you see your reflection?

My friend Barry Kolb says, "Anytime you think you have power, try ordering around someone else's dog." Real influence doesn't come from being "the boss." It comes from who you are, the way you live.

You reflect your worldview everywhere you go. As you influence those in your social network, hold a mental mirror up to your life. Look at your behavior. Think about your decisions. Consider your priorities. Diagnose your principles. Identify your values. What message do you send to others? How do you impact those around you? How are you shaping your children? Do you reflect a spiritual worldview or popular opinion?

Here's Our Prescription:

Make this your lifelong approach: Get more grounded in God's Word—and live your life accordingly. Our world is filled with secular, negative influences. Don't be one of them. Let God guide you. Become a person with eternal impact.

"...when others are troubled, needing our sympathy and encouragement, we can pass on to them this same help and comfort God has given us."
2 Corinthians 1:4 (The Living Bible)

#182 Bible View

Theme: Worldview

How does your world look?

Everyone has a worldview. It is the way you understand the world and how the world works. There are many worldviews. At one time, people thought the world was flat. If you sailed too far, they believed you would fall off the edge. Then, one day an explorer gave it a try. Everyone developed a new worldview. Your vision can change through *new information.* The Christian worldview is based on Scripture. As a believer, it drives your behavior. However, research shows many Christians do not reflect a *biblical worldview* in some areas. It is a disaster for their lives, their churches, and the future of Christianity.

Here's Our Prescription:

Commit to live a biblical worldview. How? Become a serious student of the Bible. Learn God's view for effective living. Enroll in His school of absolute truth. It is the only approach to abundant living. You maximize life when you give up all you are to receive all you can become. Let God's Word be your lens when you look everywhere.

"'You will know the truth, and the truth will set you free.'"
John 8:32 (Contemporary English Version)

#183 Friends

Theme: Fellowship

Do you have a close friend?

When I was little, I was lonely. There weren't any other kids my age in our neighborhood. For a while, I had no siblings. So, I created a pretend friend named Papo. He was always with me. Today, I am fortunate. My wife, Janet, is my best friend. Next to her there are our children, their spouses, and the grandchildren. Before they died, my parents and in-laws were great friends. Some of my colleagues at Church Doctor Ministries are good friends. A pastor in Omaha is my good friend. So is another pastor in England. Great friends are a blessing.

Do you have good friends? It is better to have a few true friends than all the acquaintances in the world.

Here's Our Prescription:

If you don't have good friends, pray for some. They are those with similar values. The best friend God has for you is Jesus. Speak with Him through prayer. Learn from Him in Scripture. Lean on Him. Then, find other believers who shine the light of Christ on you. Those friends represent your best friend, Jesus.

"...let us continue to love each other since love comes from God...."
1 John 4:7 (The Message)

#184 Loneliness

Theme: Fellowship

Do you ever feel alone?

If you have visited a nursing home, you met some lonely people. They soak up human contact like a sponge. Loneliness is all around. People can be lonely in a crowd. Some have dozens of contacts, but no relationships. Perhaps you are one of them. Are you lonely?

Here's Our Prescription:

Recognize that God is with you—always. His love is relentless—you can't escape it unless you ignore it. People touched by God's love want to share it with others. Get involved serving through your church. You will be gratified serving others and find friendship among those who work with you. This is the supernatural glue of the body of Christ. We are knit together in a special family. You were not created to be lonely. With Jesus, you are never alone. With other Christians, you are the family of God.

"He makes the whole body fit together perfectly. As each part does its own special work, it helps the other parts grow, so that the whole body is healthy and growing and full of love."
Ephesians 4:16 (New Living Translation)

#185 Group Power

Theme: Fellowship

Do you feel included?

Matt became a Christian at twenty-three. His family goes to church regularly, and he serves on a ministry team. However, as he faces issues at work, home, and church, Matt feels overwhelmed. He is not spiritually growing at the pace of his challenges. He is experiencing "spiritual slippage." Can you relate?

Here's Our Prescription:

Get involved in a small group of people who study the Bible. Discuss God's Word and its implications for everyday life. The Scripture is both simple and profound. Invest in your life by learning with others. You will never run short of biblical insights. You will experience the glue of fellowship. When Christians are together, it feels like family. Don't simply go through life; *grow* through life. Mature with others on the same journey. Don't let life's challenges outpace your faith. Be part of a growth group!

> *"Everything that was written in the past was written to teach us. The Scriptures give us patience and encouragement so that we can have hope."*
> *Romans 15:4 (New Century Version)*

#186 People-Starved

Theme: Fellowship

Are you starved?

My life's work is analyzing and helping churches. Often I see believers talking in the hallway during a Bible study. I watch others drinking coffee in the fellowship hall, then dashing off to church at the last second. I notice those hanging around with each other in the parking lot after church. These are signs of Christians starved for fellowship.

Are you? Christian fellowship is getting together with others who share the faith. Fellowship—not membership—is the glue that holds the church together. It is a gift from God.

Here's Our Prescription:

Get together with your friends, and start a group that meets regularly. Share what God is doing in your life. Celebrate birthdays and anniversaries. Share joys and concerns. Pray with one another. Design your group around opportunities for fellowship. Feed on Scripture and the feast of the fellowship that goes with it.

"How wonderful it is, how pleasant, for God's people to live together in harmony!"
Psalm 133:1 (Good News Translation)

#187 Family Feeling

Theme: Fellowship

Are you standing alone?

Did you ever meet someone who wasn't born into a family? Of course not! God puts us together. It is also why He places us in a church. It has been said, "A Christian without a church is an orphan." You are wired to be connected.

Are you in a church? Maybe you are. Yet, it doesn't feel like family anymore. Perhaps your congregation grew and added a second worship service. Now, you don't see your friends. It could be you miss the "family feeling."

Here's Our Prescription:

When churches grow, the people need small groups to build relationships. Get into a group with fellow Christians. Meet at someone's house every week or two, or once a month. Talk about what God is doing in your life. Study Scripture. Share prayer requests. Celebrate achievements. Eat some food. Get in a group and experience the "family feeling"!

"You are citizens along with all of God's holy people.
You are members of God's family."
Ephesians 2:19b (New Living Translation)

#188 Group and Grow

Theme: Fellowship

Are you in a group?

Every two weeks, Jim and eleven others meet at Bob and Sally's house. They bring snacks, talk about their lives, and study Scripture. Jim needs the discipline to study the Bible. However, he is attracted to the group because he likes the people.

Here's Our Prescription:

Find those who enjoy your hobbies and share similar values. Your affinity for one another makes your group dynamic and exciting. Don't think of it as a clique. It doesn't have to be. From a positive perspective, it is a gathering of those with similar interests. Your group can support and encourage faith and fellowship.

Your group can also reach out. We call them SEND Centers. When most people first show interest in faith, they are not "ready" for worship. The powerful platform for growth is in relationships. When you meet someone who shows interest, invite them to your SEND Center group. Help them catch the fellowship. Use an introduction to Christianity like the Alpha videos or the card game *The Gift* (experiencethegift.com). SEND Centers are "incubators" for new Christians.

"Look after each other so that not one of you will fail to find God's best blessings."
Hebrews 12:15a (The Living Bible)

#189 Outlets

Theme: Fellowship

Need an outlet?

Jim and Sue attend a very large church, almost every Sunday. They are not involved in a small group, nor do they attend an adult Sunday school class. The result? They aren't *relationally* connected with their church. They talk about how they are missing the "family feeling." Does this sound like you?

Chuck Colson once said that Christians are not supposed to be Lone Rangers. When Christians get together, they add value to each other. Church is a spiritual family like no other. Fellowship feels like family. Community makes it clear: You are never alone. When believers come together, everyone is stronger. So, plug in! John Wesley said, "The Bible knows nothing of solitary religion."

Here's Our Prescription:

Get in a group. Make it a priority. Come together regularly. Encourage one another. Share your joys. Pray for needs. Expect a great experience. Enjoy the fellowship. And, expect Jesus to show up!

"For where two or three are gathered together in My name, I am there in the midst of them."
Matthew 18:20 (New King James Version)

#190 Adversity Theme: Courage

Do you feel you're getting beaten up by life?

Discouragement, disappointment, sorrow, hurt, pain, and difficulty. Life has its challenges, even for Christians. Sadly, most difficulties come at the hands of others. You likely know this because you've been there. Ever feel like you are on the edge of giving up?

Here's Our Prescription:

Don't give up. Take time out. Recognize this: We live in an imperfect world. God didn't make it that way. We did. We still do. Christians are not perfect, but they are forgiven. Before you give up, go up—to God. Pray for understanding, encouragement, and strength. Get into your Bible. Get with trusted Christian friends. Let them wrap their arms around you. When adversity comes your way in life, it is an opportunity for God to strengthen you. And He will!

"Here on earth you will have many trials and sorrows. But take heart, because I have overcome the world."
John 16:33b (New Living Translation)

#191 Cut — Theme: Courage

Have you ever been cut?

When I was in seventh grade, I was cut from the baseball team. It was devastating. I couldn't catch, and I didn't hit very well. I was discouraged! Months later, we discovered I needed glasses. I couldn't play baseball, because I didn't see the ball very well. Who knew? What is it in your life that has you discouraged? Health? Finances? Church? Work? Loss of someone you loved? Life's challenges can drastically affect the way you think.

Here's Our Prescription:

Sometimes the real issue is too close or complex to see. Find a friend who can objectively interpret your issues -- and put them into perspective. They act as a "lens correction." God's promise: He will never cut you from His team. He will never withdraw His love and grace. Nothing can separate you from God's love. He loves you — in every circumstance. Find a Christian friend you trust. Let God use your friend to help you. God is on your team, and He is not going anywhere — ever.

"For I am convinced that neither death nor life, neither angels nor demons, neither the present nor the future, nor any powers, neither height nor depth, nor anything else in all creation, will be able to separate us from the love of God that is in Christ Jesus our Lord."

Romans 8:38-39 (New International Version)

#192 Overwhelmed **Theme: Courage**

Are you losing your grip?

Sarah was cooking dinner when the phone rang. The baby was crying, and the older kids were fighting. She listened to the bad news about her grandmother's health. Dinner started burning on the stove. Sarah was overwhelmed.

Do you ever feel that way?

Here's Our Prescription:

Take a time out! Ask yourself: "Am I *temporarily* overwhelmed?" Take a deep breath, and recognize—it will pass. Talk to someone who cares about you. What if you are constantly "overwhelmed"? Change your lifestyle. Get some help. See a Christian counselor. Get with Christian friends and read the Bible—God's "health food" for discouragement. Pray. Ask God to stand with you. Ask others to pray for you. Let God's peace heal your stress. You may be temporarily overwhelmed, but with God, you don't have to worry.

"Don't worry about anything; instead, pray about everything; tell God your needs.... If you do this you will experience God's peace, which is far more wonderful than the human mind can understand."
Philippians 4:6-7a (The Living Bible)

#193 Surprised? Theme: Courage

Are you feeling troubled?

Julie blew up: "I quit! I'm not working in this office anymore. Pastor John is just too irritable." Julie was shocked that challenges occur in ministry. When she offered to help at the church, she had unrealistic expectations. She never dreamed the pastor could be under significant stress. She quit and became part of the problem, rather than contributing to the solution. Are you surprised?

Here's Our Prescription:

Don't be naïve about church. Read your Bible. The Old Testament prophets, New Testament apostles, disciples, and Jesus Himself—they all experienced huge difficulties. Why? We are surrounded by human beings. People mess up. The solution is not in us, but in Christ. Look to Jesus, the Head of His body—the church. Persevere, with His help. God might be providing a spiritual growth process in your life. Don't be the problem. Be part of the solution! God is always on the job for you. You will get through it and will grow from it.

"Friends, when life gets really difficult, don't jump to the conclusion that God isn't on the job. Instead, be glad that you are in the very thick of what Christ experienced. This is a spiritual refining process, with glory just around the corner."
1 Peter 4:12-13 (The Message)

#194 Be Strong! Theme: Courage

Do you need encouragement?

Al wished he could simply disappear. All the pressures and stress of life were draining him, making him discouraged. In the solitude of his prayers, he silently asked for strength.

Are you facing a big test in life? Do you have a tough job? Are you dealing with difficult people? Do you privately question your abilities or your self-worth? Do you wish you were stronger? You need a shot of divine courage.

Here's Our Prescription:

Read the first chapter of Joshua. Three times God says, "Be strong and courageous." There was a time when I said, "Strong and courageous? Easy for you to say, God." My issue? I didn't realize *how God works*. This is what you should know: God *is* with you—always. His presence is promised to all believers. Jesus has won the victory. Focus on Him. Read your Bible. Receive His strength and peace. When life gets you down, God will pick you up. Jesus knows: In life, we need all the encouragement we can get!

"'This is my command—be strong and courageous! Do not be afraid or discouraged. For the LORD your God is with you wherever you go.'"
Joshua 1:9 (New Living Translation)

#195 Stand! Theme: Courage

Are you standing?

When I was a kid, they sang a song in church, "Stand Up, Stand Up for Jesus." It seemed odd: We sang it sitting down! Of course, it is more than a song. What do you do at work when you discover unethical business practices? Do you make a stand for Jesus? What if someone criticizes your faith? Do you stand up for Jesus? What if someone gossips to you about another person? Do you have what it takes to stand up against slander? What if a friend is practicing a lifestyle contrary to Scripture? Christian faith is not always easy, is it? However, you know, it's always the best way.

Here's Our Prescription:

God gives you armor—supernatural protection. It is not provided for you to simply sit around safely. It is for standing firm: for life, for others, and for what is best for our world. Your Creator gives you courage to stand up for Jesus. When you stand for Jesus, you don't have to take life's challenges sitting down!

"Put on the full armor of God so that you can fight against the devil's evil tricks."
Ephesians 6:11 (New Century Version)

#196 Dis-couraged Theme: Courage

Is your courage running on empty?

After many painful months, John lost his wife to cancer. In the process, he spent all of his savings. His son rebelled at the loss of his mother—even against God. John was discouraged. In truth, he was devastated.

Do you feel devastated? If you are discouraged, your courage is gone. Your life is running on empty.

Here's Our Prescription:

Find someone to *encourage* you—pour courage into your tank. Pray to God for help. Share your challenges with other believers. Don't let pride get in the way. Allow others to love you in Christ. Become an encourager. Lift up others with this promise in Romans 8:28: "…in all things God works for good with those who love Him…." As you encourage others, God encourages you. The presence of God is the power of encouragement. You will become a courageous Christian.

"The good man does not escape all troubles—he has them too. But the Lord helps him in each and every one."
Psalm 34:19 (The Living Bible)

#197 Relational Outreach

Theme: Outreach

Do you know how to share Jesus?

Sam has worked with Paul for five years. As a Christian, Sam would like to share his faith. However, the months slipped by, and nothing happened. Do you face this challenge? Most Christ-followers face two roadblocks when it comes to telling others about Jesus: (1) They think they have to share Bible passages and might not remember them, and (2) they fear rejection.

Jesus didn't call you to be a Bible expert, and He doesn't want you to lose a friend. He asks you to simply be a witness, like in court: "I was there; it happened to me."

Here's Our Prescription:

Has Christ made a difference in your life? If so, then you have spiritual fuel to share your faith. Share your own, personal "God stories"—what God has done for you. Start praying for an opportunity. Build a relationship. Look for an opening in the conversation. Then simply share what God has done in your life. With God's help, you can be God's messenger!

"An unreliable messenger stumbles into trouble, but a reliable messenger brings healing."
Proverbs 13:17 (New Living Translation)

#198 Don't Preach! Theme: Outreach

Would you like to talk about it?

Do you want to share your faith, but don't know how? You may be confused about what it takes. Many Christians think they have to be trained in theology. They feel they need to speak eloquently—like a preacher. Some believe it requires a command of Bible passages. Don't let any of that concern you!

Here's Our Prescription:

Faith sharing works best in dialogue with your heart. Don't overthink this. Can you hold a conversation? Are you willing to listen as well as share? Are you good at developing a relationship? Can you tell someone how God has helped you through some difficulty in your life? Do you have some "God stories" from your own experience? If you can do that, you can share your faith. You don't need a pulpit or a degree in religion. You simply need a *platform* for dialogue. Your best strength is a *relationship*. Your power is the Holy Spirit. Your mission field is those you already know. Simply tell your stories about how God has helped you.

"...you will receive power when the Holy Spirit comes upon you. And you will be my witnesses, telling people about me everywhere...."
Acts 1:8 (New Living Translation)

#199 Acceptance Theme: Outreach

Do you accept others for who they are?

When I asked several unbelievers what they thought about Christians, guess what they said? "Most Christians think they are better than me." Why would they say that? They have perfection and forgiveness confused! Would you like more help sharing your faith?

Here's Our Prescription:

Follow Jesus' example. Remember the tax collector? The prostitute? The Samaritan? The woman caught in the act of adultery? The "religious" leaders wanted to throw stones! Jesus accepted them as they were. He showed unconditional acceptance. It is called "grace." He showed love. They caught it. It changed them forever. Can you accept others as they are, even though you want something better for them? This makes a huge difference. Love is a powerful platform to share your faith. Ask God for help to accept others—like Jesus did. Show love and acceptance: They will know you are different. It is about Who is inside you. Just tell how God has changed your life—sins and all.

"'You judge in the same way that everyone else does,
but I don't judge anyone.'" –Jesus
John 8:15 (Contemporary English Version)

#200 Relate-Relationship Theme: Outreach

Can you relate?

You likely know someone who needs Jesus. And, deep down, you want to share your faith. Some become Christians through someone bringing them to worship. Others meet the Lord at an evangelistic gathering or concert. There are those who get the good news on the radio or online. Others are moved by a Christian film. However, most people meet Jesus through a relationship with a Christian—like you.

Here's Our Prescription:

Relate your faith. Focus on your *relationship* with unbelievers. Develop a deeper connection with those who are in your social network. Be honest, transparent, and real. Be yourself. When they learn you truly care about them, they will listen. Don't manipulate them into the Kingdom of God. Simply *care* for others. *Share* what faith has meant in your life. When you pray, ask the Lord to provide relationships and opportunities to share *your* faith. Don't be surprised when God answers. And, don't be shocked about how easy it is to share! People without faith are hungry for hope.

"Always be prepared to give an answer to everyone who asks you to give the reason for the hope that you have."
1 Peter 3:15b (New International Version)

#201 Bridge Events Theme: Outreach

Are you building bridges?

The famous radio commentator Paul Harvey once said, "We have drifted away from being fishers of men and have become keepers of the aquarium. We have moved from mission to maintenance." How does this happen? There are several reasons: self-focus, fear, laziness, lost passion. Perhaps we believe the lie: "It's the pastor's job." What about you? Would you like to be an effective "fisher of men and women" for Jesus?

Here's Our Prescription:

Develop a fellowship "bridge" to share God's love. Host a dinner at your house for those who don't know Jesus. Pray before you eat. Ask your guests if there is anything you can pray for them. Most people will give you something to pray for! Prayer is a brief message shared in a nonthreatening way. People are more receptive than many Christians think. Through this experience, God will rekindle your passion. You can impact someone for eternity. A relational bridge makes outreach easier.

"I'm putting you on a light stand. Now that I've put you there on a hilltop, on a light stand – shine! Keep open house; be generous with your lives. By opening up to others, you'll prompt people to open up with God…."

Matthew 5:15b-16 (The Message)

#202 Sports Talk Theme: Outreach

Are you in the game?

Two pastors were at a football game. One said to the other, "I hate football, but I love being where people are excited!" In our culture, many are interested in sports. Whether it's Little League, Monday Night Football, or March Madness, sports are a "cultural trigger."

How can you bridge sports to Jesus?

Here's Our Prescription:

Think of close friends who enjoy sports. Have a group dinner and fellowship before big games. Invite them to a Bible study followed by watching a sporting event on television. Start a conversation about a sports hero who is a devoted Christian. If Jesus were physically here on earth now, He might hang out at the gym. Why? Because He went where people were. Don't drop the ball of faith. Use sports as a bridge to introduce others to Jesus. Share your faith—and score big for God!

"You've all been to the stadium and seen the athletes race. Everyone runs; one wins. Run to win. All good athletes train hard. They do it for a gold medal that tarnishes and fades. You're after one that's gold eternally."
1 Corinthians 9:24-25 (The Message)

#203 Needs

Theme: Outreach

Can you feel the hurt?

Charlene is sixteen. She is pregnant, and the father isn't interested. Mike is serving a prison term for drug use. No one visits him. Laura is eighty-three, living in a nursing home. Does she look forward to tomorrow? Not much.

Many people are hurting in our world. Whether their pain came by their own choices or not, Jesus loves them. Most have no idea. Do you see your opportunity? You can help those who are scorned, imprisoned, and forgotten. They matter to God.

Here's Our Prescription:

Pray for them. Visit them. Your presence impacts those in pain. Share compassion and stories of what God has done in your life. Ask God to open your eyes and your heart to the needs around you. Share His love with hurting people. For those who have no one, you are the difference that makes a difference.

"I have voluntarily become a servant to any and all in order to reach a wide range of people...."
1 Corinthians 9:22 (The Message)

#204 110 Percent

Theme: Involvement

Can you do the math?

Ever hear someone say, "I want you to give 110 percent"? Coaches say it in sports. You may have heard it at work. Have you ever been asked to get involved at church?

Here's Our Prescription:

Consider God's math for your life. You might call it "the 110 percent approach." Give one hundred percent to your job and your family, with balance for rest, personal growth, and relaxation. Then give ten percent to serve God's work. You will discover a miraculous reality: The part you carve out for God, you don't really ever lose. When someone asks you to invest in God's work, think of the 110 percent formula. You can't lose. Mathematically, it seems impossible. It is a miracle.

"...give yourselves completely to God, for you were dead, but now you have new life. So use your whole body as an instrument to do what is right for the glory of God."
Romans 6:13b (New Living Translation)

#205 Pruned

Theme: Involvement

Are you hurting?

Jesus taught that He is the vine and we are the branches. Connected with Him, we produce. Then, God prunes us back—so we produce more fruit.

Do you feel like you are being pruned right now?

Here's Our Prescription:

Consider this: God may have you in a "season" that builds character and strengthens faith. Ask Him to reveal where He is taking you. When He is finished, you will be pruned, spiritually more productive. You will have greater impact on those around you. You will be a stronger representative for Christ. If life drives you to your knees, it is a good position for prayer. Ask for perspective and perseverance. You are likely in a spiritual pruning season.

"'I am the true vine, and my Father is the gardener.
He cuts off every branch in me that bears no fruit,
while every branch that does bear fruit he prunes so
that it will be even more fruitful.'"
John 15:1-2 (New International Version)

#206 Satisfaction

Theme: Involvement

Are you under-satisfied with life?

Perhaps you heard the words from that old song by the Rolling Stones: "I can't get no satisfaction." If satisfaction reflects genuine fulfillment, where do you get it?

Here's Our Prescription:

When you are involved in God's work, you produce eternal fruit. The work may be temporary, but the impact can be eternal. C.S. Lewis said, "If you can't find satisfaction in this life, it's probably because you were made for another." You can taste eternal significance by getting involved in God's work. So, when God invites you to serve, say, "Yes." You will experience the sweet fulfillment of eternal fruit. Beyond the challenge, you will discover divine satisfaction! Stay connected to Jesus!

"'Remain in me, and I will remain in you. For a branch cannot produce fruit if it is severed from the vine, and you cannot be fruitful unless you remain in me.'"

John 15:4 (New Living Translation)

#207 Success?

Theme: Involvement

What is your goal?

Imagine climbing the ladder of success. Then, you make it to the top—only to discover the ladder is leaning against the wrong wall. Is the greatest goal in your life to make a living, or to make a difference?

Here's Our Prescription:

It has been said, "The greatest use of life is to spend it on something that will outlast it." God's work is all about making a divine difference in others, a miraculous difference in our world. When you move the objective from a paycheck to divine destiny, you move from the village of success to the universe of significance. So, what will it be for you? Success is for now. Significance is forever. Choose the one that will outlast your life! Add God's work to your life, and make an eternal impact on others.

"…let yourselves be pulled into a way of life shaped by God's life, a life energetic and blazing with holiness."
1 Peter 1:15 (The Message)

#208 Legacy

Theme: Involvement

Do you have a plan?

Who will you impact a hundred years after your funeral? As a Christ-follower, you will be with God. However, what about your continued influence here on earth? It won't be about the monuments you build or the toys you accumulated. It won't have anything to do with titles, popularity, or money in a bank account. You can't take it with you. Have you ever seen a U-Haul attached to a hearse?

Would you like to invest with eternal dividends beyond the grave?

Here's Our Prescription:

Add value to others. It is called legacy living. Introduce others to Jesus. Share with them how He has changed your life. Help them explore God's Word. Adapting a Greek proverb, serving God's work is like "planting trees whose shade we know we will never sit in." You can provide a legacy that will continue long after your casket rots and tombstone fades. Direct people to Jesus while there is still time!

"...God's gift is real life, eternal life, delivered by Jesus, our Master."
Romans 6:23b (The Message)

#209 Busy?

Theme: Involvement

Is your life cluttered?

The world is filled with inventions: smartphones, Instagram, Uber. We are "blessed" with advances that, fifty years ago, few people could imagine! However, breakthroughs can also be sources of stagnation. How *much* television do you watch? How *long* do you spend surfing the Internet? Self-discipline is more important than ever.

Jesus lived a life without clutter. He knew what was important and spent His time doing God's work. Jesus was focused. How is your life?

Here's Our Prescription:

Examine your use of time. How many hours do you spend with the Lord? Is it enough? Try giving ten percent of your life to God. Instead of watching another show you will forget in a few days, spend time in prayer. Read your Bible. Serve those who are hurting. Care for the needy. Witness to those who don't know the Lord. Invest in God's Kingdom. Find the balance that works for you.

"Reverence for God adds hours to each day…."
Proverbs 10:27a (The Living Bible)

#210 Firsting

Theme: Involvement

Do you have priorities?

A priority is what you always do first. Every area of life has priorities. Finishing a task for your boss is a high priority. Cutting your grass before the kids disappear in it might be a priority, too! Your priorities reflect what is important to you. How do you choose yours? Does God influence your priorities?

Here's Our Prescription:

It is impossible to have the best priorities without consulting God's Word, the Bible. The more you allow God to speak, the better you will understand what He wants you to prioritize. As you grow spiritually, God's priorities become yours. You better understand His plan for this world. You clearly see His plans for your life. Make it a priority to spend time in Scripture. Pray to God. *Then* develop your priorities. You will discover: It is the best way to live a balanced life. Put God first. You will live life better!

"I alone know the plans I have for you, plans to bring you prosperity and not disaster, plans to bring about the future you hope for. Then you will call to me. You will come and pray to me, and I will answer you."
Jeremiah 29:11-12 (Good News Translation)

#211 Cleanliness

Theme: Excellence

Is it time to clean?

The teacher asked the third grade students to finish this sentence: "Cleanliness is next to _______." One boy raised his hand and said, "Impossible!" Does it seem like cleanliness is next to impossible at your church? Does it even make a difference? You bet it does!

We had a favorite restaurant where we ate after church. It slowly deteriorated in cleanliness. The restrooms and dining room were always dirty. That place is now out of business. The same principle holds true for your church—a dirty building is a bad reflection on God. It might keep people from returning.

Here's Our Prescription:

Don't let messiness become an obstacle for guests who come to your church. Offer to help! Pick up litter. Join with others who are dedicated to "first impression" excellence. It is not just a saying—it is a spiritual discipline: Cleanliness is next to godliness! How does that apply to your home? What about the land? The air? The oceans? Faith in God impacts everything!

"Whatever you do, work at it with all your heart, as working for the Lord...."
Colossians 3:23 (New International Version)

#212 Committed Committees Theme: Excellence

Are you on a church committee?

It was a frustrated church member who said, "A church committee is the only life form with twelve stomachs and no brain!" It sometimes feels that way, doesn't it? But not always! Some church decision makers serve very well. The key to great performance for God is a commitment to excellence. It applies to your church, your work, and your life.

Here's Our Prescription:

The next time you serve in some area at church, begin by asking about the primary purpose of the group. Make sure everyone is clear and focused. Determine that everyone is on the same page. Discuss your commitment to excellence. Establish a level of performance that will keep you from the doldrums of the typical church committee. Remember, Christ is the Head of His body, the church. Jesus is God's best. God deserves our best. Let it start with you!

"And it is my prayer that your love may abound more and more, with knowledge and all discernment, so that you may approve what is excellent...."
Philippians 1:9-10 (Revised Standard Version)

#213 Motivated for Mission Theme: Excellence

Do you feel important?

Ted Engstrom of World Vision once said, "A profit-making organization is the easiest to run. Running a volunteer organization like the church is the hardest ... you're challenging these people to difficult ministry—without pay."

Reflect on your service to God. You might help set up chairs, usher, teach a class, lead worship, share your faith, or prepare the PowerPoint content. No one pays you. Why do you do it?

Here's Our Prescription:

Spend some quiet time in prayer. Read your Bible. Ask, "What is God's mission?" Reflect on Matthew 28:19-20—"Go and make disciples." Think about your incredible privilege to serve the King of the universe. No matter how you serve, ask God to give you a commitment for excellence. You are on a mission from God. Your partnership with Jesus leads others to become friends with God. Make no mistake—you are important!

"Here we are, then, speaking for Christ, as though God himself were making his appeal through us. We plead on Christ's behalf: let God change you from enemies into his friends!"
2 Corinthians 5:20 (Good News Translation)

#214 Quality

Theme:
Excellence

What is "quality" church for you?

Bob drove home from church in silence. At home, it was Bob's teenage daughter, Mary, who broke the silence: "Is it just me, or was that sermon boring today?" It wasn't the first time a family worshipped God, went home, and had "roast preacher" over dinner.

Are you looking for excellence? Perhaps your search is closer than you think. Maybe it should begin—and end—with you. Awesome worship isn't just about the preacher or the musicians. It also depends on you as a worshipper.

Here's Our Prescription:

Get a good night's sleep. Start your day of worship with prayer. Listen to Christian music as you travel to worship. If needed, take a bathroom break before church. If it helps you pay attention, sit toward the front. Excellence in worship is nonnegotiable. God deserves the very best. Sometimes that depends on you! Trust God and grow in His love. Wouldn't it be great if everyone approached worship that way?

"And I pray that Christ will be more and more at home in your hearts, living within you as you trust in him. May your roots go down deep into the soil of God's marvelous love...."
Ephesians 3:17 (The Living Bible)

#215 Rolling or Coasting? Theme: Excellence

Are you up and down?

I love roller coasters. One minute you overlook the park. The next, you race at breakneck speed, screaming down the track. For some, roller coasters are a rush of excitement. However, your spiritual life is not intended to be a roller coaster.

Where are you in the spiritual journey? Up and down? If you are at a low point, ask yourself, "How much time am I spending in the Bible?" It was D.L. Moody who said, "The purpose of the Bible is not to change your doctrine. It's to change your life."

Here's Our Prescription:

Commit to developing holy habits. Read the Bible every day. Follow a Bible reading calendar. Get an app on your phone. Listen to worship songs in your car or while you exercise. Pursue a life of spiritual excellence. Discover God's purpose for your life. Get off the roller coaster of ups and downs. Life is already challenging enough. Whether you are up or down, let God smooth your path. Become more like Jesus.

"Imitate God, therefore, in everything you do, because you are his dear children."
Ephesians 5:1 (New Living Translation)

#216 Truth Decay

Theme: Excellence

Do you know the truth?

I saw this on a church sign: "Fight truth decay. Study your Bible every day." What about you? Are you suffering from truth decay? Do you know God's Word as much as you would like? Plato said: "We can easily forgive a child who is afraid of the dark; the real tragedy is when adults are afraid of the light." Jesus said, "You will know the truth, and the truth will set you free." Jesus is the light of the world.

Here's Our Prescription:

Read and study the Bible every day. Don't stop until you die. Pray about what you learn. Wrestle with what it means for you. Join a small group Bible study. The Scripture is God's only blueprint for living with excellence. Use a translation that speaks to you. Apply what God says about your everyday life. The Scripture is your daily dose of God's wisdom. It is power for life.

"…I am not ashamed of this Good News about Christ. It is the power of God at work, saving everyone who believes…."

Romans 1:16 (New Living Translation)

#217 Awakening

Theme: Excellence

Who are you impacting right now?

Today, Christianity is about eighty-three million times larger than when it first began. The outward movement of the church is the longest sustained endeavor in history. Do you know how it works? Consider God's math: It's called geometric progression. If you take this page and fold it fifty times, how tall would it be? It would reach from here to the sun! You are part of an enormous movement. How can you multiply your faith in others?

Here's Our Prescription:

Ask God to lead you to someone you can disciple—train, equip, and grow in the faith. Ask the person to join you for Bible study. Commit to pour your Christian life into that person. Meet regularly. Teach your disciple God's wisdom. Pray together. Serve together. Show how you live through the ups and downs of life. Demonstrate how to share the faith with others. When you invest faith in a person, you join God's longest effort in history. Multiply yourself. It is the most substantial investment of your life—and for eternity.

"Go, then, to all peoples everywhere and make them my disciples: baptize them in the name of the Father, the Son, and the Holy Spirit, and teach them to obey everything I have commanded you. And I will be with you always, to the end of the age."
Matthew 28:19-20 (Good News Translation)

#218 Gen R

Theme: Generations

Do you know someone who is *different*?

Last Christmas at church, my friend Marcia joked, "Some people today have more stuff hanging from their bodies than we have on our Christmas tree!" Every generation has distinctions. Do your children, grandchildren, or neighbors seem *different*? Does that challenge you?

Here's Our Prescription:

Don't get freaked out by the nose rings, tattoos, different clothes, or whatever. People have always expressed their uniqueness. Thank God for them! *Different* people can be open to faith in Christ! Here's how to help them: Be honest about your own Christian faith. Be real. Make Christian integrity your priority. Give the music of new generations a chance. Dress codes change. *Different* doesn't make people bad. Be a Christian friend to those who look, talk, or live differently than you. Share your faith in Jesus. Help them learn how to share their faith. God could use you to start a new Christian movement among a uniquely different group of people. An orchestra has different instruments, but in harmony, makes beautiful music.

"So then, let us aim for harmony in the church and try to build each other up."
Romans 14:19 (New Living Translation)

#219 In Your Face

Theme: Generations

Do you tell it like it is?

A man told his physician: "Well, that may be your diagnosis, but I think it was what I ate for dinner last night." It's not always prudent to tell it like it is. But, if you want to reach younger generations for Jesus, straight-to-the-point Christianity works best. They know the difference between reality and virtual reality. Most younger people don't just want to hear about Christianity. They want to experience it. Do they see it in your actions?

Here's Our Prescription:

Share your faith with those younger than you, including those in your family. Don't "beat around the bush" or worry about offending. Don't water down truth or soften the challenges you face. Be authentic. Tell it like it is. Get to the point. Speak with conviction. Be transparent because that is what works. Don't look to your church to disciple your children. You do that. Practice in-your-face Christianity with your children and grandchildren. Younger generations will respect you and respond.

"May God our Father himself and our Master Jesus clear the road to you! And may the Master pour on the love so it fills your lives and splashes over on everyone around you…."
1 Thessalonians 3:11-12 (The Message)

#220 Integrity

Theme: Generations

Do you demonstrate integrity?

Like every generation, younger people today have their strengths, weaknesses, and challenges. Our multimedia world influences them in every way. They have learned to be skeptical. Yet, they are also spiritually hungry. Many come from a world of broken marriages, broken homes, and broken dreams. They are looking for spiritual authenticity.

Do you want to impact this generation for Christ?

Here's Our Prescription:

Younger people respond to those who "walk the talk." They are not impressed with those who "play church." They want you to be real. So, don't pretend you are perfect. To effectively influence the next generation for Christ, be transparent. Be honest. Be yourself. Share how Christ makes a difference in your life, even when you mess up. Share examples about how Jesus guides you through challenges. Don't just go through the motions of "churchianity." Be real, and let them know Jesus is real.

"He (God) grants a treasure of common sense to the honest. He is a shield to those who walk with integrity."
Proverbs 2:7 (New Living Translation)

#221 Halftime

Theme: Generations

Is it halftime for you?

The eighty-five-year-old woman had her first date in fifty years. He was a fellow resident at the nursing home. Her granddaughter asked, "How did it go?" She replied, "Well, I had to slap his face twice." "Did he get fresh?" asked the granddaughter. "No," the woman replied, "I had to make sure he was still alive!"

Are you getting older? Every game is won in the second half.

Here's Our Prescription:

If you are older, you have a legacy message to share. God has traveled life with you. You have a unique opportunity to serve God and impact others. How? Value this part of your life. Stay strong in your faith. Share your spiritual wisdom and experience with others. You will make an eternal difference in someone's life. Think beyond the armchair, television, or fishing pole. There's nothing wrong with those—but what about God's call? Life isn't over at fifty, sixty-five, or eighty-five! In God's service, it might be just beginning! Focus on opportunities with eternal dimensions.

"There is a right time and a right way to do everything...."
Ecclesiastes 8:6 (Good News Translation)

#222 Reprioritizing

Theme: Generations

Are you looking for more?

Carl Sandburg said, "There is an eagle in me that wants to soar, and there is a hippopotamus in me that wants to wallow in the mud." You likely know someone who has enjoyed "success." Their mortgage is paid off, and their kids are through college. They have graduated beyond the "daily grind." Perhaps you are one of them. Congratulations on your success!

Here's Our Prescription:

Move from success to significance. God's work is divine, eternal, and changes the destiny of others forever. Speak freely! Sharing your faith story is an investment that will outlast your life. If you are in the second half of life, focus on fulfillment. It is not about toys, being first, or becoming popular. It is sowing seeds of God's love in others. If you share how God has worked in your life, you will have eternal impact. Let God's spirit speak through you. The rewards are out of this world!

"...Live freely, animated and motivated by God's Spirit."
Galatians 5:16a (The Message)

#223 Generational Distinctiveness

Theme: Generations

Do you have hope for the future?

I remember when our son, Jonathan, came home excited. "Tomorrow's wild hair day at school!" The school actually invited the kids to do something weird with their hair. My son bleached his brown hair blond. Our son! Do you have kids?

Here's Our Prescription:

Lighten up! Every generation needs to express itself. They need to be distinctive to be different. It is likely a declaration of independence. It is human nature. It also occurs in the church. Don't get uptight about changes in "delivery systems" your church uses. Give "different" music styles a chance. It is called "contextualization." It is why Jesus came in "the flesh." When you see a young person in church with wild hair, what is important: to be upset about his hair, or rejoice that he is there, hearing about Jesus? The message must never change. Delivery systems always do.

> *"...I will pour out my spirit on everyone...your old people will have dreams, and your young people will see visions."*
>
> *Joel 2:28 (Good News Translation)*

#224 Interface

Theme: Generations

Are you interactive?

I remember when I quit playing video games with our daughter, Laura. I just couldn't take the constant defeat. Now Laura has daughters of her own. Guess what? There is a whole new generation of technology! Each generation experiences an increasingly interactive world. Some of these changes have permeated the way churches worship. Does that bother you?

Here's Our Prescription:

Accept reality. We live in an interactive world. So, interact with your children or grandchildren. If you have children at home, don't just lecture. Lead spiritual discussions. Give them the opportunity to process the practical side of faith. Above all—be a friend your children can trust. Share your personal faith in Jesus. Show the love of Christ to them. Interact with them for Kingdom influence. Don't rely on Sunday school or Vacation Bible School to disciple your children. These are great ministries, but if you want your kids to grow up active in the faith, you need to disciple them.

"...You should be like one big happy family, full of sympathy toward each other, loving one another with tender hearts and humble minds."
1 Peter 3:8 (The Living Bible)

#225 Grief

Theme: Compassion

Is someone you know hurting?

The casket arrived at the church. Hundreds of police officers and their families came to say goodbye to the officer who had been shot. It was an incredibly difficult time for the young family.

Have you ever heard, "It only takes a spark to get a fire going"? It is true, especially when it comes to reaching out to others with the love of Jesus.

Here's Our Prescription:

Be proactive. Help families grieving from the loss of a loved one. Send a card or gift. Go beyond: Be a friend. Provide a listening ear. Just say, "I am so sorry for your loss." Add, "I am praying for you." Continue: "Let me know if there is anything I can do to help." Your acts of compassion will lead others to help. Hurting people see the love of Jesus through you. Be living proof that His love never fails. Hope is eternal. Faith is real.

"Love is patient and kind; it is not jealous or conceited or proud; love is not ill-mannered or selfish or irritable; love does not keep a record of wrongs; love is not happy with evil, but is happy with the truth. Love never gives up; and its faith, hope, and patience never fail."
1 Corinthians 13:4-7 (Good News Translation)

#226 Kids Having Kids

Theme: Compassion

Can you help?

Debbie is a high school senior with hopes and dreams. Yesterday, she discovered she is pregnant. The result? College plans are on hold. Her family is impacted. She is in a different category than her friends. They are pursuing college or careers. She feels all alone.

Children having children is a challenge. They need compassion. It is an opportunity for God's unconditional love.

Here's Our Prescription:

Every challenge is an opportunity for ministry. Your response, as a Christian parent or friend, is to offer support and understanding. Your encouragement—and nonjudgmental attitude—can show someone like Debbie the love of Jesus. Don't mentally shake your head and look the other way when someone is troubled. See it as a moment "pregnant" with opportunities to share God's love, forgiveness, and healing. Everyone sins and falls short of God's expectations. Have a heart like Jesus for those who are troubled.

"He will feed his flock like a shepherd. He will carry the lambs in his arms, holding them close to his heart."
Isaiah 40:11a (New Living Translation)

#227 Go to Jail

Theme: Compassion

Do you really want to help?

Get out of church, and go to jail. Today, many Christians are reaching out to those who are imprisoned. Most believers live a few minutes from a police station. Still, many who are incarcerated go unreached by believers. Have you ever been in prison? It is true: You have a captive audience!

Here's Our Prescription:

Think about all the broken people in prisons who could receive the good news about Jesus. Pray about joining a ministry that brings the love of Jesus to those behind bars. Get some of your friends together and learn how to reach out to prisoners. Jesus had compassion on those society ignored. He knew: Their hearts were ready for help. You will experience how Jesus truly sets people free.

"'Master, what are you talking about?... And when did we ever see you sick or in prison and come to you?' Then the King will say, 'I'm telling the solemn truth: Whenever you did one of these things to someone overlooked or ignored, that was me – you did it to me.'"

Matthew 25:37-40 (The Message)

#228 Youth Compassion

Theme: Compassion

Do you know who said this about young people?

"Our youth have bad manners, contempt for authority, and disrespect for older people. Children nowadays are tyrants. They contradict their parents, chatter before company, gobble their food, and tyrannize their teachers."

Who said that? It was Socrates—a long time ago. In every generation, young people challenge adults. If you are an adult, perhaps you have forgotten that you, too, went through challenges, fears, and "experiences" as a kid. Now *your* children or grandchildren are going through it. So, what will you do?

Here's Our Prescription:

Have compassion on them. Work hard to understand their perspective. Focus on the fruit of the Spirit called patience. Show them you care enough to listen. Seek first to understand and then to be understood. That is what Jesus did. Be a friend at a time when kids need it most! And point them to the Savior, every chance you get, by what you say, what you do, and who you are.

"One day children were brought to Jesus in the hope that he would lay hands on them and pray over them. The disciples shooed them off. But Jesus intervened: 'Let the children alone, don't prevent them from coming to me. God's Kingdom is made up of people like these.'"

Matthew 19:13-15 (The Message)

#229 Hermititis

Theme: Compassion

Are you only focused on YOU?

It is a malady that challenges many Christians. It subtly attacks when you decide to keep God's love all to yourself. You become a spiritual hermit. Isn't it great that Jesus didn't have that attitude? When Christ-followers get all wrapped up in themselves, they make very small packages. Put them in a self-centered church, and they reduce God's impact on the world Jesus died to save.

Here's Our Prescription:

Reach out to someone in need. Show compassion to those who are hurting. Don't let spiritual hermititis lead you to retreat, ignore, or hide. Share God's love with others through your service, encouragement, and willingness to engage those who are hurting. Pray, and ask God to show you someone in need today. Reach out to them. Pray with them. Share your faith. Touch their lives with God's love. Become a giant disciple with quiet discipline.

"So, chosen by God for this new life of love, dress in the wardrobe God picked out for you: compassion, kindness, humility, quiet strength, discipline."
Colossians 3:12 (The Message)

#230 Compassion for Your Pastor

Theme: Compassion

Who is in charge?

Elder Bob was pointing out the church's most influential people to the new pastor: "That is Deacon Jones—he runs the meetings. There is Mrs. Hamel; she runs the Sunday school. Over there are the Goldsmiths; they run the nursery. And, see that guy? That is Lloyd. He has run off the last four pastors!"

Being a pastor is a tough job. Some encouragement from you will go a long way to help.

Here's Our Prescription:

Pray for your pastor every day—starting today. When a great message makes an impact, let your pastor know—on your way out the door. Send a note of encouragement to your pastor twice a month—starting this month. Offer to serve—without being asked. Do something special and nice for your pastor's spouse—every month. Become a champion of compassion for your pastor. You can make a big difference in many small ways.

"Appreciate your pastoral leaders who gave you the Word of God."
Hebrews 13:7a (The Message)

#231 Hope Dealer

Theme: Compassion

Do you share your hope?

You hear a lot about serious challenges at schools. Sometimes it's a drug bust. Maybe it's child abuse or a gun in a locker. Do you ever wonder how many kids go to school worried? Thank God for a Christian like you! Why? You are a dealer in hope. You recognize there is uncertainty in the world. However, you also know who owns the world. You can also tap the strength God gives every day.

Here's Our Prescription:

Share your hope in Christ with the next generation. Children face many fears. Teach them powerful Scripture, like Psalm 23 and Romans 8. Hope, through Christ, is powerful! It provides fuel to get through the challenges of life. When you demonstrate hope in children, they become filled with hope—hopeful! Make this your spiritual routine: Encourage young children. Point to the power of Christ. Be a dealer in hope.

"I alone know the plans I have for you, plans to bring you prosperity and not disaster, plans to bring about the future you hope for."
Jeremiah 29:11 (Good News Translation)

#232 Soul Mates　　Theme: Prayer

Do you have a soul mate?

One of my heroes is the Apostle Paul. He is the picture of perseverance. He faced betrayal. He was beaten and stoned. Imprisoned. Slept in chains. He was shipwrecked. And eventually, he was murdered for his faith. Yet, he never faced life alone. Paul knew Jesus was with him. During his ministry, he traveled and served with numerous companions. When he faced difficulties, he trusted God and leaned on his friends. They were spiritual support partners.

Here's Our Prescription:

Find some "soul mates"—personal partners in your journey of faith. There is nothing noble about facing spiritual challenges by yourself. Jesus went to the garden to pray, but He wasn't there alone. Develop a circle of prayer partners. Ask a few close friends to regularly pray for you. And, you pray for them. Start a small group. Study the Bible together. Share challenges with each other. Persevere through life's difficulties—together. Your prayer partners are soul mates for your life.

"Dear friends, let us love one another, because love comes from God. Whoever loves is a child of God and knows God."
1 John 4:7 (Good News Translation)

#233 Prayer Power — Theme: Prayer

Why do you pray?

Someone once said, "God's *promises* show his heart: Your *prayers* show yours!" In Matthew 6:8, Jesus says, "Your Father already knows what you need before you ask Him." So, why pray? God doesn't need to be informed. He already knows everything. He doesn't need to be moved. He already has mercy. This is the point: Your prayers are a statement of faith, an expression of your personal relationship with the King of the universe.

Here's Our Prescription:

Dedicate yourself to an improved prayer life. God doesn't care about the arithmetic of your prayers—how many; or the rhetoric—how eloquent; or the geometry—how long; or the music—how sweet; or the logic—how phrased; or the method—how orderly. All God is looking for is a sincere and trusting conversation. You can do that. Talk with God today. He is always listening, waiting for you to demonstrate your relationship.

"Your Father already knows what you need before you ask Him."
Matthew 6:8b (Good News Translation)

#234 Translator Theme: Prayer

Do you know what to say?

Do you feel like you don't know what to pray? The Bible says that even if you are uncertain how to pray, the Holy Spirit will translate whatever you pray into perfect language. The story is told of a Scottish Presbyterian pastor who prayed long prayers with lofty language. A woman in the congregation spoke up and got right to the point: "Just call him Father, and ask Him for something."

Here's Our Prescription:

Plan today to move your prayer life to the next level. You don't have to be a theologian to talk to God. Just speak like a friend. Have a conversation, like a child to a loving dad. Pray with confidence. You can't make a mistake. The Holy Spirit will translate your words. You can't lose—unless you choose not to pray.

"In the same way the Spirit also comes to help us, weak as we are. For we do not know how we ought to pray; the Spirit himself pleads with God for us in groans that words cannot express. And God, who sees into our hearts, knows what the thought of the Spirit is; because the Spirit pleads with God on behalf of his people and in accordance with his will."
Romans 8:26-27 (Good News Translation)

#235 Sharing Prayer Theme: Prayer

Do you ever share prayer?

Have you been asked to pray in public and your blood pressure soared? Have you wanted to pray with a friend but didn't have the courage? Are you too hung up on what others might think to pray in a small group—afraid you will make a mistake?

Perhaps you should be like the young girl saying her bedtime prayers. She was reciting the alphabet. Her mother asked what she was praying. She said, "I didn't know what to pray, so I just said all the letters. God can put it together!" That's right, God *can*, and *will*, put your prayer thoughts together.

Here's Our Prescription:

For that coward in you who really wants to pray: Get over it! Take a deep breath, trust God, get out of His way, and just pray. For most things in life, practice makes perfect—except with prayer. God doesn't care about perfect. Let go, and let God!

"This is your Father you are dealing with, and he knows better than you what you need. With a God like this loving you, you can pray very simply."
Matthew 6:8 (The Message)

#236 Praying for the Lost Theme: Prayer

Do you pray for those who are unbelievers?

Sir Isaac Newton once said, "With my telescope I can look millions of miles into space, but in prayer I can get closer to God in heaven than all the telescopes on earth." Do you know some unbelievers in your social network? Do you wish they knew the Lord?

Here's Our Prescription:

Make a list of those you know who don't know the Lord. Ask God for the discipline to pray for them every day. Put your list on your bathroom mirror—or someplace you will see it every day. You may not be called to be a missionary. You may not be an evangelist. Yet, you can pray. When Jesus looked at the crowds, He told the disciples to pray to the Lord of the harvest to send workers into His harvest. So, pray to the Lord. The mission always begins with prayer. The disciples must have prayed for the Lord to send workers, because He answered their prayer: He sent them. And He might send you!

"'So pray to the Lord who is in charge of the harvest; ask him to send out more workers into his fields.'"
Matthew 9:38 (New Living Translation)

#237 Fast Track Theme: Prayer

Have you ever tried fasting?

In Copenhagen, there is a statue of the inviting Christ by Albert Thorwaldsen. The day he molded the clay for that statue, the figure of Christ was looking toward heaven with His arms stretched upward. However, during the night, a dense mist rolled in from the sea. The next day, Jesus' head was bowed and His arms were lowered. The artist left it that way, claiming, "If you want to see the face of Christ, get on your knees."

Scripture speaks about prayer. It also references fasting. Fasting is about going without food, or certain foods, or anything that is normally important. God uses fasting and prayer to move us toward humility, repentance, spiritual renewal, and mission.

Here's Our Prescription:

Try the disciplines of fasting and prayer. It could make a spiritual difference in your life. Take the "fast" track! And pray as you go.

> *"When you practice some appetite-denying discipline to better concentrate on God, don't make a production out of it. It might turn you into a small-time celebrity but it won't make you a saint. If you 'go into training' inwardly, act normal outwardly....God doesn't require attention-getting devices. He won't overlook what you are doing; he'll reward you well."*
> *Matthew 6:16-18 (The Message)*

#238 Basics Theme: Prayer

Do you know the basics?

Revival, renewal, awakening: There is a divine desire to see more people become believers. A return to God is the hope, dream, and wish of many. If you want to see it happen, it means you will go back to the basics. The legendary football coach Vince Lombardi said to his players, "This is a football." He went back to the basics. They won many games. Would you like to see more people "won" to Christ?

Here's Our Prescription:

Get back to the basics: Spend time with Jesus. Pray often. Ask Him to show you His character. Ask for wisdom to understand how He thinks: His passion, His will—for you, your life, your family, and our world. Bill Bright once said, "Prayer doesn't always lead to revival, but revival always follows prayer." Basics: Vince Lombardi wanted to win games. Christians want to win the world. How important is that? It's not rocket science. Just ask God: "Bring revival, beginning with me."

"God...delights in genuine prayers."
Proverbs 15:8 (The Message)

#239 Fear Factor Theme: Faith

Are you crippled by fear?

Have you ever felt God was leading you to do something, but you were hesitant to go forward? Have you ever been invited on a mission trip but didn't take the plunge? Have you ever been asked to lead a group at church, but said "no"? If so, you may have been crippled by fear.

Fear is often the reason Christians miss out on God's blessings.

Here's Our Prescription:

Read your Bible every day. It is like taking spiritual vitamins! Make Isaiah 41:10 your motto. God says, "Do not be afraid—I am with you!" You can believe that! Trust God. Pray for stronger faith. Perfect love—God's love—takes away any reason to be afraid. And, when you lose your fear, share your victory. From your experience, others learn to trust God. They will see the power of God's love. They will be healed from the fear that cripples.

"There is no fear in love; perfect love drives out all fear."
1 John 4:18a (Good News Translation)

#240 Bob Christ — Theme: Faith

Did you ever have the passing thought: "Is He real?"

When I was young, in Sunday school, I learned a lot *about* the Savior. I learned His name was "Jesus." I thought His last name was "Christ." Then I learned that "Christ" means "the Chosen One of God." I learned facts, but never developed a personal relationship. It was "academic" faith. Do you struggle with that as well?

Pretend for a moment the Lord's real name was Bob. So, he might be called Bob Christ. I know, it sounds weird. It is so common. Is it because you know others who have the name Bob? In Jesus' day, His name was common, like "Bob" today!

Here's Our Prescription:

Pray. Ask Jesus to be more *real* in your life. Don't make Him academic. Believe like a child. Remember: It is not *what* you know, but *Who.*

"My response is to get down on my knees before the Father, this magnificent Father who parcels out all heaven and earth. I ask him to strengthen you by his Spirit – not a brute strength but a glorious inner strength – that Christ will live in you as you open the door and invite him in. And I ask him that with both feet planted firmly on love, you'll be able to take in with all followers of Jesus the extravagant dimensions of Christ's love. Reach out and experience the breadth!"

Ephesians 3:14-18 (The Message)

#241 What a Friend Theme: Faith

Is Jesus your friend?

Ever sing, "What a Friend We Have in Jesus"?

Former first lady Rosalynn Carter wrote: "I think that God will never send/ A gift so precious as a friend/ A friend who always understands/ And fills each need as it demands/ Whose loyalty will stand the test/ When skies are bright or overcast/ Who sees the faults that merit blame/ But keeps on loving just the same/ Who does far more than creeds could do/ To make us good, to make us true/ Earth's gifts a sweet contentment lend/ But only God can give a friend."

Here's Our Prescription:

Talk with Jesus every day. Work at developing a relationship with the Lord. Let Him become real in your life. Think of Jesus as God. He is! Look to Him as Ruler of the Universe. He is! Consider Him the Head of the church. He is that, too! However, put this truth in your mind, on your heart, and in your life. Jesus is your friend.

"...I call you friends, because I have made known to you everything I heard from my Father."
John 15:15b (New Century Version)

#242 Talk, Talk, Talk Theme: Faith

Are you talking with Jesus?

When our daughter was young, our house phone didn't ring much. When she turned sixteen, that changed. Some days I felt like a receptionist! Isn't it amazing, when little girls mature into young ladies, how they develop relationships with many conversations? Isn't it wonderful that teenagers now have cell phones? Well, maybe! Or, sometimes!

So many people are constantly on their phones. I saw four young adults at a restaurant. None of them were talking with each other. They were all texting on their phones!

It is not that way with you and Jesus. Prayer is His conversation line.

Here's Our Prescription:

In the busyness of your life, schedule a heart-to-heart talk with Jesus every day. You can have a "thought prayer" as you drive in your car—just don't close your eyes! Make prayer an everyday conversation. Speak, but also listen. He hears your words and knows your heart. Have a heart-to-heart talk.

"...whoever calls out to the Lord for help will be saved."
Acts 2:21 (Good News Translation)

#243 Listen! Theme: Faith

Are you listening?

My wife claimed I didn't listen to what she said—at least, I think that is what she said! Good listeners are not only popular. After a while, they actually know something! God gave us two ears and only one mouth. Perhaps we should spend twice as much time listening as talking!

In the Bible, God says, "Be still and know that I am God!"

Here's Our Prescription:

Do you want to grow your faith? In the fast pace of life, be still and read your Bible. Use a modern translation that speaks your "heart language." (It is the language of your dreams.) Meditate on what Scripture says. Apply it to your life. Pray through the issues raised in the Bible passage. Then, be quiet and listen! And when you hear the heartbeat of God, you will be refreshed by His Breath of Life! God will change your life! Can you hear Him? Are you listening?

"Be still, and know that I am God. I am exalted among the nations, I am exalted in the earth!"
Psalm 46:10 (Revised Standard Version)

#244 Evangelistic Stroke Theme: Faith

Can you talk?

It is like some Christians have had an evangelistic stroke. They can talk about anything else but God. They tell jokes and stories. They go on and on about baseball. They even talk about their in-laws. Yet, when it comes to faith, they get spiritual lockjaw. Is that you?

Perhaps you don't practice enough. After all, my stories are best when I tell them for the third time.

Here's Our Prescription:

The best way to heal an evangelistic stroke is exercise. Practice sharing your faith. Share what God has done in your life. Tell your "God story"—how the Lord changed you. Rehearse with a Christian friend. Isn't that the way Jesus taught His disciples? When you feel comfortable, share your God story with an unbeliever. Talk about what God has done. It is a little scary at first, but God will work in an amazing way! And, it gets easier every time you share.

"...I thank my God through Jesus Christ for all of you, because the whole world is hearing about your faith."
Romans 1:8 (Good News Translation)

#245 In, Out, Old, or Up? Theme: Faith

In what direction are you growing?

Are you ingrown, outgrown, oldgrown, or grownup? Ingrown faith is when you are only concerned about yourself. You become so heavenly minded, you are no earthly good! You don't care about others. Outgrown faith isn't healthy, either. You become spiritually fat and lazy. You think you know it all. You have the "been-there-done-that" syndrome. You have no room to learn, energy to serve, or openness to change. Oldgrown faith is stuck: "We've always done it that way." You make God look out-of-date.

Here's Our Prescription:

Ask God to lead you to grownup faith. It is a lifelong process. Feed on Scripture. Chuck Swindoll said, "A sign of maturity is when you go from a thick skin and a hard heart to a tough skin and a soft heart." When it comes to faith, it is good to grow, as long as you are growing up! God's wisdom will grow in you and accomplish more than you can imagine.

"To him who by means of his power working in us is able to do so much more than we can ever ask for, or even think of: to God be the glory in the church and in Christ Jesus for all time, forever and ever! Amen."
Ephesians 3:20-21 (Good News Translation)

#246 Fresh Food — Theme: Outlook

Are you hungry for God?

The little girl saw the Bible on the coffee table and asked, "Whose book is that?" Her mother replied, "Well, honey, that is God's book!" The girl responded, "We ought to give it back; we certainly aren't using it."

It doesn't matter if you've read the whole Bible a hundred times. Every time you read it, you become a better person. God gives you new insights, a better outlook on life.

Here's Our Prescription:

Set aside time each day—make it a regular discipline. Go online and look at the wide variety of study Bibles. Check out those with helpful study notes. Get the translation that works best for you. Watch how God renews and builds your spiritual strength day by day. Consume God's Word. He provides spiritual food for life.

> *"God means what he says. What he says goes. His powerful Word is sharp as a surgeon's scalpel, cutting through everything, whether doubt or defense, laying us open to listen and obey. Nothing and no one is impervious to God's Word. We can't get away from it—no matter what."*
> *Hebrews 4:12-13 (The Message)*

#247 Motivation — Theme: Outlook

How are you motivated?

The story is told of the frog who was stuck in a pothole. His frog friends tried to coax him out, but he couldn't jump far enough. They went to get some food, but when they returned, he was out and on the side of the road. They asked how he got out. He said, "A semi came down the road, and I had to." He obtained a whole new level of motivation!

How do you get energized for serving God and others?

Here's Our Prescription:

Don't let guilt motivate you. The ability to serve God and help others is a privilege. As a Christian, you have been honored to join hands with the King of the universe. You are elevated to the status of an ambassador for Jesus. Real energy to serve God doesn't come from rules, threats, fear, or guilt. It is motivated by love: God's love for you, demonstrated in Jesus.

"We love because God first loved us."
1 John 4:19 (Good News Translation)

#248 Absolutaphobia — Theme: Outlook

Do you have an opinion?

It is called absolutaphobia: a fear of *absolutes*. *Leadership* magazine once reported that 48 percent of Americans believe there is no truth that is always right. One out of two people believe in "relativism"—all kinds of truth. It is one thing to be open-minded, but not so much your brains fall out!

Christianity is based on God's Word. Christians know what they believe and believe what they know. A man said, "I don't know what the Bible says, but I think..." The Christian faith isn't based on opinion, but revelation—from God. His truth is absolute.

Here's Our Prescription:

As a Christian, you will reflect a lifestyle of learning from God's Word. Put your opinions on the shelf. Discover truth as God sees it. Get in a group Bible study. Believe what God says. It is *absolutely* the right thing to do. God is *absolutely* right. You can *absolutely* count on Him!

> *"You're going to find that there will be times when people will have no stomach for solid teaching, but will fill up on spiritual junk food – catchy opinions that tickle their fancy. They'll turn their backs on truth and chase mirages. But you – keep your eye on what you're doing;...keep the Message alive; do a thorough job as God's servant."*
> *2 Timothy 4:3-5 (The Message)*

#249 Anemic? Theme: Outlook

Do you feel spiritually weak?

Where are you right now in your journey of faith? If you are at a low point of Christian enthusiasm, consider how much time you are spending in the Bible. God's Word is like food. If you don't "eat," you get weak. Are you spiritually anemic?

Here's Our Prescription:

The Scripture is a roadmap to change your life… and for eternity. Here are some holy habits: Attend a Bible class once each week. Read your Bible every day. Get a Bible calendar. Start a reading program. Get a Bible reading app on your phone. Listen to Scripture in your car. Use a modern translation that speaks to your heart. Let God strengthen you—fill up on His Word. Feeding on God's Word doesn't make you overweight. It makes you spiritually fit.

"By your words I can see where I'm going; they throw a beam of light on my dark path. I've committed myself and I'll never turn back from living by your righteous order. Everything's falling apart on me, God; put me together again with your Word."
Psalm 119:105-107 (The Message)

#250 Multiplication Theme: Outlook

Are you a multiplier?

A Chinese proverb says: "If you want one year of prosperity, grow grain. If you want ten years of prosperity, grow trees. If you want a hundred years of prosperity, grow people." Jesus grows people. He said, "Go, make disciples." You are called to be a multiplier. Reinvest your faith in someone else. You are a discipler. You equip others to make disciples. You become an exponential multiplier!

Here's Our Prescription:

Grow people. Multiply yourself by encouraging and discipling others.

Live the amazing, eternally productive life the way Jesus did: by making disciples who become disciplers. Your influence can extend beyond your life, your geography, your imagination. How? By raising up others. Be fruitful and multiply!

"Jesus, undeterred, went right ahead and gave his charge: 'God authorized and commanded me to commission you: Go out and train everyone you meet, far and near, in this way of life, marking them by baptism in the threefold name: Father, Son, and Holy Spirit. Then instruct them in the practice of all I have commanded you. I'll be with you as you do this, day after day after day, right up to the end of the age.'"
Matthew 28:18-20 (The Message)

#251 Life Beyond Ordinary Theme: Outlook

Are you excited?

When Margaret's husband died, she decided not to cave into life's circumstances. She went on a short-term mission trip to Tibet. After ten days, she came home with a new mission. She went to college and studied animal husbandry. She learned to raise yaks. She moved to Tibet, started a yak farm, and makes them available to the poor at cost. In the process, she shares about Jesus. She is called the Yak Lady of Tibet. She has experienced life beyond ordinary.

It is a big world. God has an extraordinary imagination when it comes to serving the greatest cause in eternity. Do you wake up every day and ask God what amazing opportunities He has for you? They are there for you! Are you looking for them?

Here's Our Prescription:

List your dreams to serve God. Declare to the Ruler of the universe, "I'm available." Let God excite you about His great cause. When you work for eternal consequences, you discover life beyond ordinary. Take an amazing journey you will never regret.

"The Lord says, 'I will teach you the way you should go; I will instruct you and advise you.'"
Psalm 32:8 (Good News Translation)

#252 In My Opinion Theme: Outlook

What do you think?

Ever hear, "Well, if you ask me…"? Opinions are dangerous—they jump to conclusions. The real danger? Those who never change their opinions never correct their mistakes. This issue surfaced with Adam and Eve: They had a higher opinion of themselves than of God. "Never mind what God said; let's eat the fruit!" And all hell broke loose—literally!

Here's Our Prescription:

Subordinate your thinking to what God directs. Submit your desires to prayer. Pray each day what Jesus prayed in the Garden of Gethsemane: "Not my will, but Your will be done." Live it: You want what God wants for you. Put that prayer at the front end of every decision, at the back end of every conclusion, and in the middle of every judgment. Make Scripture your guidebook. You will travel where God wants you to go. And, you will be glad you did.

"He (Jesus) went a little farther on, threw himself face downward on the ground, and prayed, 'My Father, if it is possible, take this cup of suffering from me! Yet not what I want, but what you want.'"
Matthew 26:39 (Good News Translation)

#253 Authority **Theme: Integrity**

Who rules your life?

The word "authority" comes from the word author. The author is the originator. The originator is the creator. The Creator of all things is God. Jesus said, "All authority in heaven and on earth has been given to Me." Yet, among humans, the greatest challenge is control—a lack of trust. It is like the church board member who joked: "It takes a two-thirds majority to overturn the will of God!"

Here's Our Prescription:

Focus your life on a high level of integrity. That requires you to live under submission to authority. That means following the Author. When Jesus said that all authority had been given to Him, it was no joke. God was in Jesus Christ bringing peace, forgiveness, and new life to the whole universe. If you are challenged by that authority, get reacquainted with the Author. He will change your priorities, your attitude, your hope, your life, your family, your world. The surprise? You will find peace. Why? God is watching.

"We preach the word of God with sincerity and with Christ's authority, knowing that God is watching us."
2 Corinthians 2:17b (New Living Translation)

#254 Living above Reproach

Theme: Integrity

Do you reflect God's truth?

How are you impacted by God's truth? Is it simply because you hear preaching? The visible impact of the Bible doesn't become more powerful because you read a verse. The influence of Scripture comes through when your friends see your commitment and integrity. When others hear spiritual "truth" from you, they can say, "That is your opinion. It is true for you, but not for me." However, when they see the results of God's truth in you, it becomes contagious.

Here's Our Prescription:

Live what you believe. Make what you believe determine how you act. How you act is what you believe. Live above reproach. Live so no one can poke holes in the way you live. That is a tough job! No one is perfect. The good news? You live under God's grace—His gift of forgiveness for you. Ask Jesus for help to put your faith into practice each day. The best message you can send to your friends is how God has changed the way you live.

"Strive for righteousness, godliness, faith, love, endurance, and gentleness. Run your best in the race of faith, and win eternal life for yourself; for it was to this life that God called you when you firmly professed your faith before many witnesses."
1 Timothy 6:11b-12 (Good News Translation)

#255 Walk or Talk? Theme: Integrity

Do you walk the talk?

Some people won't listen to the truth about Jesus. Why? They don't see any change in the lives of believers. Integrity is to walk the talk, live the life. We aren't perfect—but forgiven. Yet, we can always get better at living our convictions.

Here's Our Prescription:

Don't just live what you preach. Preach what you live. You will become more effective. After all, a bald man can't sell hair restoration oil! Study your Bible. Strengthen your Christian lifestyle. Pray for strength and direction every day. Ask a Christian friend to serve as your accountability partner. Help each other "walk the talk." Never underestimate the importance of integrity. God will use you to make an impact on others and our world! What if you mess up? Demonstrate remorse, and thank God for forgiveness.

"The life you see me living is not 'mine,' but it is lived by faith in the Son of God, who loved me and gave himself for me."
Galatians 2:20 (The Message)

#256 3D View — Theme: Integrity

How do you see?

Some Christians struggle. They don't yet have a biblical worldview—the Christian approach about how believers see the world. Are you influenced by the world more than God's truth?

Here's Our Prescription:

If you want to make a spiritual impact on others, here's a plan. Develop a 3D worldview: **D**ivinely **D**irected **D**ecisions. Read your Bible every day. Join a Bible study group. Discuss God's truth with others. Let God's Word drive your decisions. Subordinate your own desires to God's direction. **D**ivinely **D**irected **D**ecisions will revolutionize you, your family, your church, and the world! Operating from a biblical worldview provides hope for renewal, revival, and the future. So 3D your life: Make **D**ivinely **D**irected **D**ecisions, and watch the impact God will make in you and through you!

"What you should say is this: 'If the Lord is willing, we will live and do this or that.'"
James 4:15 (Good News Translation)

#257 Like a Rudder Theme: Integrity

Did you hear about…?

The Bible says the tongue is like a rudder of a ship: small, but powerful. Used the wrong way, tongues can steer God's people and their churches toward disaster. Gossip wrecks relationships. Jesus teaches that we are to confront one another in love.

Here's Our Prescription:

Read Matthew 18:15-17. It says you should talk privately to the person who offended you. If that doesn't work, go again and take a Christian friend. And if that doesn't work, then you take it to the church or church leaders. All of this is done face-to-face. It is the approach of speaking the truth in love. If you want harmony, improve the way you use your tongue. If someone offends you, follow the Lord's loving approach. It will transform your relationships and increase the health of your church.

> *"…think of a ship: big as it is and driven by such strong winds, it can be steered by a very small rudder, and it goes wherever the pilot wants it to go. So it is with the tongue: small as it is, it can boast about great things. Just think how large a forest can be set on fire by a tiny flame! And the tongue is like a fire. It is a world of wrong, occupying its place in our bodies and spreading evil through our whole being."*
> *James 3:4-6a (Good News Translation)*

#258 Lookin' Good! Theme: Integrity

How is your character?

The Bible says our character ought to be "above reproach." You don't want to give the appearance of sin. You don't want to give people the temptation to think badly of you. Abraham Lincoln said, "Character is like a tree and reputation like its shadow. The shadow is what we think of it; the tree is the real thing." Your character—who you are when no one is looking—casts a shadow on everything you do, all you think and say, everywhere you go. That shadow reflects your reputation.

Here's Our Prescription:

Cast a shadow of Christian character. Read your Bible. Develop a biblical lifestyle. Ask God to mold you. Strong character is made by what you *stand* for, but a poor reputation is the product of what you *fall* for.

"Keep your eyes on Jesus, who both began and finished this race we're in. Study how he did it. Because he never lost sight of where he was headed—that exhilarating finish in and with God—he could put up with anything along the way: cross, shame, whatever. And now he's there, in the place of honor, right alongside God. When you find yourselves flagging in your faith, go over that story again, item by item, that long litany of hostility he plowed through. That will shoot adrenaline into your souls!"
Hebrews 12:1b-3 (The Message)

#259 Will or Want? Theme: Integrity

Be careful what you wish for!

Are you more focused on what *you* want or what *God* wants? Walt Kallestad says, "Dare enough to do, and care enough to be, what is *best*, not what is *easiest*." That means submitting your desires to God's priorities.

Here's Our Prescription:

Have you ever been caught *doing* something great for God? That is OK, but perhaps you should focus more on *being* someone great for God. Read Scripture. Learn more about the character of God, how God thinks. Look at what God wants. Identify *His* priorities and purposes. Pray that line in the Lord's Prayer, "Your will be done, on earth, just as it is in heaven." When you focus on what God wants, you will discover the power of purpose. What if everyone did that?

> *"We're able to stretch our hands out and receive what we asked for because we're doing what he said, doing what pleases him. Again, this is God's command: to believe in his personally named Son, Jesus Christ."*
> *1 John 3:22-23 (The Message)*

#260 Among the Multitudes Theme: Alive and Growing!

Do you remember the COVID-19 pandemic?

When the Centers for Disease Control fears there will be an epidemic, they isolate the carriers. If they are quarantined, the disease won't spread. The devil also tries to isolate: not for good, but for evil. It is the strategy of divide and conquer.

God builds faith when you are among multitudes of believers. A Jesus epidemic is a good thing! Years ago, when my son, Jon, was young, I took him to Promise Keepers. It was a gathering of enthusiastic Christian men. We were encouraged by seeing so many who were excited about Jesus. Enthusiastic believers are contagious! Did you know the word "enthusiasm" comes from the words "in God"?

Here's Our Prescription:

Get together with large groups of believers. It is a faith movement strategy. Think about when Jesus fed the five thousand! When you worship among the multitudes, you are reminded: You are *never* alone!

"And Peter said to them, 'Repent, and be baptized every one of you in the name of Jesus Christ for the forgiveness of your sins; and you shall receive the gift of the Holy Spirit….' So those who received his word were baptized, and there were added that day about three thousand souls."
Acts 2:38, 41 (Revised Standard Version)

#261 Mountaintop Experience

Theme: Alive and Growing!

Have you been to the mountain?

Peggy said, "This has been a mountaintop experience." For her, the conference was spiritually invigorating. The concept comes from the Bible. Moses got the Ten Commandments on the mountain. Jesus went up the mountain with Peter, James, and John. Jesus gave the Sermon on the Mount.

Here's Our Prescription:

Attend mountaintop spiritual experiences. They will increase your spiritual growth. You will never be the same. There are countless numbers of Christian conferences, workshops, concerts, and worship events. Take a short-term mission trip out of your comfort zone. You will be "susceptible" to the Holy Spirit. Climb the mountain with Jesus! The multitudes of Christ-followers will ignite your fire for God.

"Moses went up Mount Sinai, and a cloud covered it. The dazzling light of the Lord's presence came down on the mountain. To the Israelites the light looked like a fire burning on top of the mountain."
Exodus 24:15-17a (Good News Translation)

#262 What a Trip!

Theme: Alive and Growing!

Are you ready to stretch?

As my wife and I entered the West African church, we heard the three thousand believers worshipping. The air was electrified with the presence of the Lord. Their enthusiasm and intensity touched our hearts, stretched our horizons, and changed our lives. I vowed that I would expose others to this incredible experience.

Ever been on a mission trip? Or worship at a megachurch? When you are among multitudes, God stretches your vision. We all live under the same sky, but we don't all have the same horizon.

Here's Our Prescription:

If you haven't been in a large crowd of Christ-followers, make a visit to a large church. Or attend a conference of excited believers. Go to a Christian concert. Or sign up for a short-term mission trip. Move out of your comfort zone—so you are more open to God. Go where God's Kingdom is growing, where people are on fire. Give one hundred percent and get two hundred fifty percent back! It's the best stretch you will ever make!

"You're blessed when you're at the end of your rope.
With less of you there is more of God and his rule."
Matthew 5:3 (The Message)

#263 Stuck in Neutral?

Theme: Alive and Growing!

Are you growing?

Do you feel like you are in a rut? Sooner or later, it happens to everyone. Someone once said the only difference between a rut and a grave is the dimensions. It was Winston Churchill who said, "To improve is to change, and to be perfect is to change often." Yet, some Christians say, "Change? Who said anything about change?" Yeah, it sometimes feels like "we've always done it that way."

Here's Our Prescription:

Once a year, plan a spiritual retreat. Take inventory of your spiritual life. How is your faith compared to a year ago? Are you stuck in a spiritual rut? What about your worship attendance? Prayer life? Bible study? Your service to others in God's name? Where is your peace? How is your joy? Add it up. Are you stuck in neutral on your spiritual journey? If it is time for *change*, get into God's Word. Pray regularly. Rediscover the power of worship. Sometimes it takes guts to leave ruts.

"Make a careful exploration of who you are and the work you have been given, and then sink yourself into that. Don't be impressed with yourself. Don't compare yourself with others. Each of you must take responsibility for doing the creative best you can with your own life."
Galatians 6:4-5 (The Message)

#264 Adult Infant

Theme: Alive and Growing!

Are you growing?

I talked to a man who said he had twenty-five years of experience as a Christian. But the more we talked, it sounded like he had only one year of Christian experience twenty-five times. He never matured as a Christian. He was physically an adult, but lived like a spiritual infant. The Bible says you are to mature in Christ, the Head of the church. You are supposed to think the same way He thinks. How does that occur?

Here's Our Prescription:

Get into regular Bible study in a group. Privately read Scripture every day. Christian growth is a process, not an event. It never ends. You are constantly growing, learning, experiencing, and developing your relationship with Jesus. Schedule regular getaways for spiritual growth. Plan them in advance, and guard them as a priority. Don't simply fill up on academic information. Spend time in prayer. Seek spiritual transformation. Let the Holy Spirit guide you.

> *"'Not by might, not by power, but by my Spirit, says the Lord…you will succeed because of my Spirit….'"*
> *Zechariah 4:6 (The Living Bible)*

#265 Devotion

Theme: Alive and Growing!

Are you "devoted" to Jesus?

The words "devoted" and "devotion" come from the same idea. To be "devoted" means you are dedicated, very loving, loyal, and faithful. How do you get there from here? How do you become a more committed follower—a stronger believer in your Savior?

Here's Our Prescription:

The Word of God feeds your soul the way food feeds your body. Without a good, regular diet of Scripture, your faith becomes weak. A weekly appearance in worship is not always enough. Be devoted! Read a portion of the Bible each day. Find a translation that is easy to understand. Start with the Gospels—the first four books of the New Testament. Or, try reading one Psalm each day. Keep a journal of your readings and how they impact your daily life. If you do this, you will grow spiritually stronger. Challenge your friends at church to do the same. Start a Bible study group. Ask God to turn it into a movement. A strong church is the result of those who are spiritually deep. If you are devoted to Jesus, let it show! God's Word is powerful!

"Your word, O LORD, will last forever; it is eternal in heaven."
Psalm 119:89 (Good News Translation)

#266 Main Event

Theme: Alive and Growing!

Do you need a lift?

When I was a seminary student, I led our youth group to a national gathering held in a large stadium. I still remember sitting on the fifty-yard line, with the stands completely filled around me. As darkness fell, everyone lit a candle, and Billy Graham led us in a prayer of commitment. It was a long time ago, but I remember it. It was a spiritual main event in my life.

Have you ever been to a large conference or gathering? It makes an incredible impact seeing all those other Christians. The friends you make and the growth you experience are immeasurable.

Here's Our Prescription:

Find upcoming events or gatherings near you. Watch for Christian teaching conferences or music concerts. You could organize an excursion for other church members. It is an incredible time investment that grows you spiritually. Do yourself a favor. Visit big spiritual events: to worship, learn, and grow. Sometimes, to grow more, you need to get away. You will prosper from spiritual growth.

"Do yourself a favor and learn all you can; then remember what you learn and you will prosper."
Proverbs 19:8 (Good News Translation)

#267 Break Out!

Theme: Friendliness

Are you stuck in a routine?

Take this quiz: Have you sat in the same seat at church so long it has worn into the shape of that part of your body? Do you tend to greet the same people at church every week? Are you uncomfortable with a new worship song you don't know? Are you religiously married to the "old hymnal" or a certain instrument? If so, you could be in a rut. Is that spiritually healthy?

Church isn't supposed to be reduced to a weekly routine. Worship is where you stretch, praise, learn, grow, and exercise faith. Honestly: What, really, is sacred about "the way we've always done it"?

Here's Our Prescription:

Get this straight: Effective Christianity has two absolutes: The content never changes. The delivery systems must. If you have become religiously comfortable, challenge yourself to grow in "faith." Greet a new face. Say hello to your friends, and move out to find first-time guests. Say goodbye to your favorite seat. Worship from a new perspective. That new song? Let yourself grow! Break out of your rut. You will be amazed how exciting faith can be!

"Sing a new song to the Lord!"
Psalm 96:1a (Good News Translation)

#268 Fishing

Theme: Friendliness

Are you fishing?

A fisherman returned after a fruitless eight hours. Not one fish! "Did you have a bad day?" someone asked him. "Yep, I didn't have one fish jump into my boat," he grumbled. Fish aren't going to jump into your boat! So, what do you do? Jesus calls you a "fisher of men and women" for the Kingdom. Invite them to worship? You are asking them to jump into the church boat. God's strategy is that you go to people, not expect them to come to you. Jesus said, "Go, make disciples."

Here's Our Prescription:

Some of Jesus' disciples were fishermen. They used nets. When you "fish" for people, you have to work the net. Think of those who don't know Jesus. They are in your personal network. Rather than waiting for them to "magically" appear at church, you can be church to them. Your relationship is your net. Invite unbelievers to a meal. Introduce them to Jesus. Cast your net.

"Walking along the beach of Lake Galilee, Jesus saw two brothers: Simon (later called Peter) and Andrew. They were fishing, throwing their nets into the lake.... Jesus said to them, 'Come with me. I'll make a new kind of fisherman out of you."
Matthew 4:18-19 (The Message)

#269 Friendly Fire?

Theme: Friendliness

Are you airing dirty laundry?

Marvin brought a friend to church. As they sipped coffee, Lance approached and said, "Hey Marvin, did you hear about the pastor having dinner with Mary, the church secretary?" The Bible is clear about gossip. Your tongue is a sharp weapon. It kills potential relationships with unbelievers.

Gossiping about fellow church members will turn off visitors and unbelievers. Why would they want to spend time with people who slander others? Becoming the object of gossip is the last thing they need.

Here's Our Prescription:

Flee from gossip. Confront gossipers in love, as the Bible says. God restores broken hearts all over the world. Don't let gossip keep others from hearing the *good news* at your church. Instead, "gossip" the Gospel—God's good news about Jesus.

"Keep away from profane and foolish discussions, which only drive people farther away from God."
2 Timothy 2:16 (Good News Translation)

#270 Welcome Mat

Theme: Friendliness

Are you friendly to those far from God?

If I visited your church, would I find the people friendly? Those who like people are people other people like. Those who are searching for God often return to a church because they find it friendly. Relationships are powerful!

I worked with a church where the longtime members said it was friendly, but the new members said it was unfriendly. How could that be? The members were friendly—with each other! On Sundays, they formed holy huddles with their friends.

Here's Our Prescription:

Become a "welcome mat." Look for the stranger, the newcomer, the person all alone. Make it your ministry every time you attend worship. Relationships are the powerful platform to grow the Kingdom. Churches are not automatically friendly. They become friendly one person at a time. Why don't you start?

"...because of his (God's) deep love and concern for you, you should practice tenderhearted mercy and kindness to others."
Colossians 3:12a (The Living Bible)

#271 Be a Friend

Theme: Friendliness

Are you reaching out?

Ever hear someone say, "Children are meant to be seen and not heard"? I've got a powerful theological response to that: Baloney! I get it from the Bible, where Jesus scolded His disciples for keeping the children from Him. Are you friendly toward adults, but indifferent toward kids?

Here's Our Prescription:

Adopt a young person in your church or in your neighborhood. Be a friend. Show interest. Nurture them toward Jesus. Send encouraging notes. Point them to helpful Scriptures. Most of all, listen and learn. Let them know they matter to God. Henry Blackaby said, "...the next generation of great leaders is already evolving, but today's adults may be too preoccupied to notice." So, reach out: You could be mentoring the next influential Christian leader!

"'Let the children alone, don't prevent them from coming to me. God's kingdom is made up of people like these.'"
Matthew 19:14 (The Message)

#272 Levels of Friendship

Theme: Friendliness

Are you a friend?

There are two levels of friendship. One is an inch deep and a mile wide. You have lots of friends, but the relationships are shallow. The other level is a mile deep and a few inches wide. Those are the few people for whom you would give your life. This kind of friend is one who steps in when the whole world runs away.

Whether you realize it or not, there are people all around you who really need a close friend. It may be someone at work or school. Perhaps it is the person who lives next door. Some think a church primarily grows through programs. It doesn't. It grows through the power of relationships. Christianity is a relational movement.

Here's Our Prescription:

Look around—who can you name, right now, who needs a friend? Friendship is the perfect platform to share your faith with another person. It is your opportunity to introduce them to your friend, Jesus. His relationship is a universe wide and an eternity deep.

"And now I give you a new commandment: love one another. As I have loved you, so you must love one another. If you have love for one another, then everyone will know that you are my disciples."
John 13:34-35 (Good News Translation)

#273 The Friendly Risk

Theme: Friendliness

Are you a risk-taker?

Sometimes you have to take a risk to show you care. My wife has two aunts that look alike. One is widowed. The other is married—and I had heard her husband was in the hospital. I saw the one with the husband and decided to take a risk—except I got the two aunts confused. So, I asked, "How's your husband doing?" She said, "He's dead." I said, "Oh, my goodness, I hadn't heard. When did he die?" She replied, "In World War II." Wrong aunt! Sometimes there is a risk when you try to care.

Here's Our Prescription:

Take a deep breath, trust God, and take the risk. Be friendly and care about others. Step out with your faith, even when it's risky. It's worth it. Jesus did it for you. Dare to show you care!

"'So do not be afraid of people…. Those who declare publicly that they belong to me, I will do the same for them before my Father in heaven.'"
Matthew 10:26a, 32 (Good News Translation)

#274 Conqueror Theme: Decisions

Who is your hero?

Everyone loves a conqueror. They become heroes: Robin Hood, Batman, even Zorro! Yet, we often put hope in our own abilities. Think about the Titanic. As it left, someone said, "Not even God could sink this ship!" The Titanic was sort of a floating, modern Tower of Babel, a human expression of grandiose technology. And it sank.

Here's Our Prescription:

Do you want to experience victory beyond human frailty? Do you want to conquer the challenges of life? Do you want your faith to impact your community? Then get back to the basics. Get back to Christ. He's the conqueror. He said, "I will build my church, and not even the gates of hell will prevail against it." To conquer tomorrow, face life today with Jesus.

"Trust in the LORD with all your heart. Never rely on what you think you know."
Proverbs 3:5 (Good News Translation)

#275 Ready? Theme: Decisions

Are you prepared?

You can be brilliant, yet not prepared for tomorrow. My brother-in-law worked for a funeral home. His job was to collect dead bodies and bring them to the funeral home. Some of them weren't prepared for tomorrow. They died without faith in Jesus.

Do you know the Lord? Are you prepared for eternity? Is Jesus your personal friend, Savior, and Lord? Are you prepared for today, tomorrow, *and* eternity? Death is a reality. Why? There is a glitch in life called sin. There is only one way it is repaired: forgiveness, through Jesus Christ. Are you ready? If not, are you ready to get ready?

Here's Our Prescription:

Don't waste another minute! As kids we said, "Ready or not, here I come!" That is what Jesus is saying to you right now. Ready or not, He is coming! Will He find Himself in your heart? If so, you are ready for eternity. My brother-in-law was ready.

"...in all these things we are more than conquerors through him who loved us. For I am sure that neither death, nor life, nor angels, nor principalities, nor things present, nor things to come, nor powers, nor height, nor depth, nor anything else in all creation, will be able to separate us from the love of God in Christ Jesus our Lord."
Romans 8:37-39 (Revised Standard Version)

#276 Willpower **Theme: Decisions**

How is your willpower?

John D. Rockefeller said, "An individual's highest fulfillment, greatest happiness, and widest usefulness is to be found in living in harmony with God's will." If you want fulfillment, happiness, and usefulness, do what God wants. However, how do you know what God wants for you?

In the Garden of Gethsemane, facing the horrific crucifixion, Jesus prayed, "Not my will, however, but Your will be done." The Lord's Prayer says, "...Your will be done on earth as it is in heaven."

Here's Our Prescription:

Pray. It is what Jesus did and what you can do. Pray every day: "Lord, show me what you want." Pray before you take that job, buy that car, marry that person. Pray before you worship. Pray before you serve. Pray when you face a challenge. Ask God to direct you according to what *He wants* for you. The Bible guarantees: He will guide you—if you let Him.

"Remember the LORD in everything you do, and he will show you the right way."
Proverbs 3:6 (Good News Translation)

#277 Consumerism Theme: Decisions

Are you a shopper?

Some people don't want to know the will of God in order to *do* it. They just want to know what God wants in order to *consider* it! Why? We live in a world of choices. We are trained to be consumers: Get what you want, buy what you like, grab the gusto, get comfortable. It's an "all-about-you" culture. It is subconscious and hard to resist.

When you face challenges, a *consumer* mentality can subtly impact your choices. It occurs when you make decisions influenced by what *you* want, rather than by what *God* wants. How do you make decisions? Are they based on what is comfortable or easy? Are they determined by habits? Have you ever said, "But we've always done it that way"?

Here's Our Prescription:

Change the way you make decisions. How do you know what God wants? Be a student of the Bible. Consult a more seasoned Christian. And, most of all, be willing to do what God wants. What if everyone did that?

"Be careful, however, that the exercise of your rights does not become a stumbling block…."
1 Corinthians 8:9 (New International Version)

#278 Opinionitis — Theme: Decisions

What is your view?

It is called opinionitis: blindness of the heart and inflammation of the attitude. This disease infects all of us: Christians, whole churches, even denominations. It occurs when opinions rule over truth. A Sunday school teacher asked the class how they thought angels do the will of God. One kid said, "They do it immediately." Another said, "Diligently." Another said, "With all their hearts." Then one kid said, "I think they just do it without asking any questions!" When your opinions are on the same level as God's will, it fractures the power of God's truth.

Here's Our Prescription:

Learn from preaching, teaching, discussions, and decisions. Put everything through the lens of God's truth. Sort out opinions from the facts. Read Scripture every day. Pray. Stick to God's will and stamp out opinionitis, beginning with you!

"Don't love the world's ways. Don't love the world's goods. Love of the world squeezes out love for the Father. Practically everything that goes on in the world – wanting your own way, wanting everything for yourself, wanting to appear important – has nothing to do with the Father. It just isolates you from him. The world and all its wanting, wanting, wanting is on the way out – but whoever does what God wants is set for eternity."
1 John 2:15-17 (The Message)

#279 Driven Theme: Decisions

What drives you?

Management expert Peter Drucker said, "If you don't know what business you're in, you're about to go out of business." Imagine a Burger King or Starbucks saying, "We are in the plumbing business." Sound silly? Our research shows that more than fifty percent of Christians don't know the primary purpose of the church!

What drives you? *Tradition* is the living faith of the dead. *Traditionalism* is the dead faith of the living. Traditionalism focuses on familiar approaches that are no longer effective. Jesus had tough words for religious traditionalists. Fulfilling God's purpose always takes priority over tradition.

Here's Our Prescription:

Jesus said that His purpose was to seek and save the lost. Put God's purpose first. Focus on Jesus' mission. Make God's business your concern. God will make your concern His business.

"Then Pharisees and scribes came to Jesus from Jerusalem and said, 'Why do your disciples transgress the tradition of the elders? For they do not wash their hands when they eat.' He answered them, 'And why do you transgress the commandment of God for the sake of your tradition?'"
Matthew 15:1-3 (Revised Standard Version)

#280 Church on Fire — Theme: Decisions

How is your passion for God?

Late one night, a church caught fire. Jeff saw his neighbor watching from his porch. He said, "Harry, I didn't know you were interested in the church." Harry said, "I'm not. I've just never seen a church on fire!"

A friend once told me, "Any person who wants to set people on fire must first be burning!" Are you on fire for God? Will Rogers prayed, "Lord, let me live until I'm dead."

Here's Our Prescription:

If your spiritual life has cooled off, ask God for new life. Ask Him to excite you about what He is doing. The word "enthusiasm" comes from two words: "in God"! And, it is caught more than taught. Pray. Ask the Holy Spirit to kindle in you a fire to spread the good news about Jesus. You could be the spark to start a spiritual revolution! Catch fire for Jesus!

"'Didn't we feel on fire as he [Jesus] conversed with us on the road, as he opened the Scriptures for us?'"
Luke 24:32 (The Message)

#281 Celebrate Each Other Theme: Celebrate!

Are you filled up?

One Bible in your mind is worth a dozen on your shelf! I have asked many Christians why they aren't involved in Bible study. They say: "It's boring," "It's over my head," "I don't find it helpful," "I don't have time." Is that you?

Here's Our Prescription:

Join a small group Bible study. You will get to know other Christians and learn more about God's Word. You can share joys, like birthdays and anniversaries. You can also talk about challenges, like pain and suffering. You will experience fellowship with refreshments and personal stories. You can celebrate victories, God's healing, and answered prayers. You will experience God's love for one another. You can pray for one another. The glue of fellowship will bring you together as you study the Bible. You will never call Bible study boring again!

"Let the peace of Christ keep you in tune with each other, in step with each other."
Colossians 3:15 (The Message)

#282 Laughter

Theme: Celebrate!

How often do you laugh?

I was working with a church in California. Some of the older people said, "The new pastor tells too many jokes." However, the younger people said, "We love the pastor's preaching. He even tells jokes!" What about laughter in church? I'm amazed how many people sing "Joy to the World," yet they act like they were baptized in vinegar!

Humans are the only living creatures endowed with laughter! We all see too much sadness on the nightly news, in newspapers, and among our friends. If Jesus is "good news," can you laugh in worship?

Here's Our Prescription:

Don't ignore the seriousness of sin. However, rejoice in God's forgiveness. If the pastor accentuates a point by telling a joke, let yourself laugh! Chances are your face won't crack. Do you have unchurched friends? Let them know: Your faith in Jesus brings joy to your world. And He will bring joy to others through you.

"...you are the source of my happiness. I will play my harp and sing praise to you, O God, my God."
Psalm 43:4b (Good News Translation)

#283 Good News/Bad News Theme: Celebrate!

Do you have good news to share?

The airplane pilot announced: "I have good news and bad news. The good news is: We are making excellent time. The bad news is: We are lost!" Isn't that just like life? Good news and bad news. It is that way for Christians as well! The bad news? We are all sinners. The good news? God provided Jesus Christ, who died so we are forgiven. The best news? Jesus rose again, and we have eternal life.

Here's Our Prescription:

Think about what you say to your friends. Do you consider they might need to hear some good news? Here is the best news: "God loves you. God wants to forgive you and empower you with joy." Think about your conversations. Do *others* hear *good* news from you? You *are* good news to your world! Just share what God has done for you. Share how the Lord has made a difference in your life. You *do* have great news to share!

"But how can people call for help if they don't know who to trust? And how can they know who to trust if they haven't heard of the One who can be trusted? And how can they hear if nobody tells them?"
Romans 10:14 (The Message)

#284 Attitudinally Challenged?

Theme: Celebrate!

How is your attitude?

Do you sometimes find worship a drag? Is the music dull? Is the preaching boring? Does the worship seem long? Would you like to give your opinion to the worship leader or pastor? Time out! Ask yourself: How open are you to God? *You* may be the issue about how much you get out of worship! The value you receive is in direct proportion to your hunger for God. It is an issue of attitude.

Here's Our Prescription:

Have a talk with the person in the mirror. Examine your own attitude. What you bring to worship impacts what you take away. Do you have great expectations as you attend worship? Do you *really* believe God will touch your life? Ask God for an attitude where you celebrate and sing, not sit and sour. You may have something to lose and everything to gain!

"It's who you are and the way you live that count before God. Your worship must engage your spirit in the pursuit of truth. That's the kind of people the Father is out looking for: those who are simply and honestly themselves before him in their worship. God is sheer being itself– Spirit. Those who worship him must do it out of their very being, their spirits, their true selves, in adoration."
John 4:23-24 (The Message)

#285 Music

Theme: Celebrate!

Are you listening?

Ever notice how many different kinds of music are on your radio? Or on Apple Music? Ever wondered what makes music "Christian"? It's not the tempo, the volume, the style, or the instruments. It is the content! The message is what ultimately makes music "Christian."

Here's Our Prescription:

Consider what you listen to as you get ready for work or when you clean the house. Christian music provides an enormous lift to your day. Every Christmas I get the same present from my wife: satellite radio in my car. I listen to one station: "The Message." You, too, can praise God, simply by turning on the radio! Tune in to your favorite Christian radio station. You will fuel your soul with a message to celebrate! In the "traffic jams" of life, let Christian music lift you higher.

"...Praise God in his holy house of worship, praise him under the open skies; Praise him for his acts of power, praise him for his magnificent greatness; Praise with a blast on the trumpet, praise by strumming soft strings; Praise him with castanets and dance, praise him with banjo and flute; Praise him with cymbals and a big bass drum, praise him with fiddles and mandolin. Let every living, breathing creature praise God! Hallelujah!"
Psalm 150:1-6 (The Message)

#286 Do It!

Theme: Celebrate!

Are you drifting?

Some Christians are like wheelbarrows. They are not much good unless they are pushed. In worship, if you snooze, you lose. Must you be pushed to express yourself in church? Do you cringe when others start to shout, lift hands, or clap?

Here's Our Prescription:

Try the PUSH method: "Praise Until Something Happens." You will discover that something always happens! Think about this: "Impression without expression leads to repression." Don't repress God's Word when it touches you! Immerse yourself in God, and He will immerse Himself in you. If you don't feel like singing, sing anyway! If the people around you start clapping, join them! Let the spirit of worship touch your heart, your head, your soul. Let go and let God. PUSH: Praise [God] Until Something Happens!

"But the time is coming and is already here, when by the power of God's Spirit people will worship the Father as he really is, offering him the true worship that he wants. God is Spirit, and only by the power of his Spirit can people worship him as he really is."
John 4:23-24 (Good News Translation)

#287 Prepare!

Theme: Celebrate!

Do you worship well?

Do you find yourself criticizing the worship team, choir, or worship leader? After church, do you have roast preacher for lunch? Do you complain to your friends about boring worship? Do you wonder, "Why do I bother to go?"

Here's Our Prescription:

If your church doesn't already do it, ask them to print next week's sermon topic in advance. Meditate on that subject all week. Think and pray about it with anticipation and preparation. Pray for those who lead worship. Get a good night's sleep the night before church. Attend worship with God on your mind. Make worship your priority. Leave the bad attitude at the door. If you are challenged to pay attention, sit up front. Give God every opportunity to speak into your life. Be open to what He wants for you. God will make your worship an awesome experience. Do your part for maximum impact!

"Come, let us bow down and worship him; let us kneel before the Lord, our Maker! He is our God; we are the people he cares for, the flock for which he provides."
Psalm 95:6-7a (Good News Translation)

#288 Get Real

Theme: Relationships

Would your friends describe you as authentic?

Do you ever put on a "church face"? I heard about a family that argued in the car all the way to church. The brother was mad at his sister, and the sister was nagging her brother. Mother was irritated with both. Dad was driving the car, and his family was driving him nuts! When they arrived at church, everyone smiled and spoke pleasantly as they made their way to worship.

Here's Our Prescription:

When you talk to an unbeliever about your faith, do you make it sound like "peaches and cream"? Or, do you tell it the way it is? Do you share how God helps you with the struggles, disappointments, and pains of life? Church isn't a country club of saints. It is a hospital for sinners. So, get real. If your relationships aren't authentic, your witness won't go very far. God is real. Be real about life and God.

"Happy are those who remain faithful under trials, because when they succeed in passing such a test, they will receive as their reward the life which God has promised to those who love him."
James 1:12 (Good News Translation)

#289 EGO

Theme: Relationships

Are you an egomaniac?

Ken Blanchard said "ego" stands for "edging God out." The world says your worth is tied to *what you do*. God says your value is reflected in *who you are*. I have a friend with low self-esteem. Unfortunately, she believes her value is in what she does, how well she does it, and how much she does. God thinks more of her than she thinks of herself!

Here's Our Prescription:

When you base your value on what you accomplish, your relationship with God suffers. So does your relationship with others. Jesus said, "I am the Vine, you are the branches" (John 15:5). When you are connected to the Vine, Christ is in you. Your *value* is related to God's love for you. Real accomplishment is *ability stripped of doubt*. Why? You have Jesus. Jesus has you. That is what makes you so valuable! If you were the only person on earth, Jesus would have still died—just for you! Don't edge God out!

"The fear of human opinion disables; trusting in God protects you from that."
Proverbs 29:25 (The Message)

#290 Family

Theme: Relationships

Are you part of the family?

On their deathbed, many people say they wish they had spent more time with their family. No one says, "I wish I'd gone to the office more." In the rat race of life, people often fall apart. However, God has designed two environments for your health and growth. Relationally, He puts you in a birth family. Spiritually, He provides a church family.

Both families are the glue that holds life together when everything else falls apart. In church, that glue is called fellowship. According to God's plan, you receive unconditional acceptance. Both families are important for your spiritual growth. Your families train you to serve God in this world.

Here's Our Prescription:

Get involved in family fellowship with other Christians. Be family to one another. Serve God according to your spiritual gifts. When you serve, you experience your divine value. Your church family is the glue that holds you together, even beyond your home. Celebrate love, forgiveness, and fulfillment. Share the good news about Jesus.

"In the assembly of all your people, LORD, I told the good news that you save us. You know that I will never stop telling it."
Psalm 40:9 (Good News Translation)

#291 Untouchables

Theme: Relationships

Can you name some people you don't like?

Who is in *your* prejudice file? Is it homeless people? Lawyers? Politicians? People who phone and try to scam you? My friend Paula knows a guy who is gay. Can she still be a friend? If not, how will she ever reach him for Jesus?

A balcony person stands above everyone else, making judgments and criticizing. A fellow traveler comes alongside others. The traveler meets people where they are, accepts them as they are, and loves them for who they can become – with Jesus.

Here's Our Prescription:

Repent of your prejudices. Ask God to keep you strong in your convictions, but compassionate in your heart. Jesus didn't pontificate from the balcony. He did it from a cross for you and for others. He calls for repentance, but does it in love. He does it as a traveler. Jesus died for untouchables like us.

"It is a difficult thing for someone to die for a righteous person. It may even be that someone might dare to die for a good person. But God has shown us how much he loves us – it was while we were still sinners that Christ died for us! By his blood we are now put right with God; how much more, then, will we be saved by him from God's anger!"
Romans 5:7-9 (Good News Translation)

#292 Love Test?

Theme: Relationships

What is your reaction?

Do you know someone who has made a big mistake? Perhaps they fell into adultery? Or got caught stealing at work? Or became addicted to drugs? Or got divorced? Are you offended? Are you uncomfortable, knowing God expects you to love that person? This could be the greatest challenge to your faith!

In John 21, Jesus asked Peter to care for people. Yet, He didn't ask, "Do you love them?" The truth is, sometimes you do, and sometimes you don't! Jesus asked Peter, "Do you love Me?" Yet, it is not only about what Jesus *said*. It is what He *did*.

Here's Our Prescription:

Hate the sin; love the sinner. That is what Jesus did. It is what being a follower of Jesus is all about. That goes for you, too, if you have made a big mistake. Can you accept forgiveness? Love Jesus. Be restored. Reach out. Forgive others.

"Live creatively, friends. If someone falls into sin, forgivingly restore him, saving your critical comments for yourself. You might be needing forgiveness before the day's out. Stoop down and reach out to those who are oppressed. Share their burdens, and so complete Christ's law. If you think you are too good for that, you are badly deceived."
Galatians 6:1-3 (The Message)

#293 Ugly Ducklings

Theme: Relationships

Are you throwing stones?

Did you ever hear the story of "The Ugly Duckling"? One was totally different from the rest. He was an outcast. Then he finally got accepted. That is a summary of the Christian faith. Sin is a sickness. Through Jesus, you receive forgiveness. In forgiveness, you find acceptance. You are not perfect. Sin is sin. It is all bad. You are broken. Yet, in that brokenness, you are healed. Through Jesus, you receive divine acceptance. Through forgiveness, you have a new level of openness.

Do you have the love of Jesus for the ugly ducklings of this world? If not, perhaps the real issue is your own brokenness.

Here's Our Prescription:

Ask for forgiveness. Experience God's grace. Pray for humility. Offer forgiveness. Live in acceptance. Develop relationships. Reach out to someone today.

"Make this your common practice: Confess your sins to each other and pray for each other so that you can live together whole and healed. The prayer of a person living right with God is something powerful to be reckoned with."
James 5:16 (The Message)

#294 Loneliness Restored

Theme: Relationships

How are your relationships?

Did you hear about the three men who were shipwrecked? A genie appeared and offered one wish each. One man said, "I want to see my family." He was gone. The next man said, "I miss my work." He was gone. The third man said, "I'm lonely. I wish my friends were here!" How are your relationships in the stormy seas of everyday life?

Is loneliness a challenge for you today?

Here's Our Prescription:

Loneliness is restored by loving relationships. Schedule time with one of your children. Spend a weekend with your spouse—without a plan. Find a Christian friend and study Scripture. Spend some quiet time with the God of love each day. Pray. Allow the Lord to speak to you. Loving relationships may be closer than you think!

"Better to eat vegetables with people you love than to eat the finest meat where there is hate."
Proverbs 15:17 (Good News Translation)

#295 No Bones about It Theme: People

Where do you fit in the church?

There are four kinds of bones in the body of Christ, the church. Wishbones spend their time wishing someone else would do the work. Jawbones do all the talking but little else. Knucklebones knock everything anyone tries to do. And then there are Backbones—they lift the load and get God's work done.

Are you aggravated by Wishbones, Jawbones, or Knucklebones? Focus on this: God made you to be active in your church. Do you hear God's call to be a Backbone?

Here's Our Prescription:

Remember Jesus' teaching? He is the Vine. We are the branches. When you are connected to Jesus, you produce fruit. Every Christ-follower is called to be a Backbone. Experience fulfillment through serving God. Your church needs you. Be a Backbone in the body of Christ!

"I appeal to you therefore, brethren, by the mercies of God, to present your bodies as a living sacrifice, holy and acceptable to God, which is your spiritual worship. Do not be conformed to this world but be transformed by the renewal of your mind, that you may prove what is the will of God, what is good and acceptable and perfect."
Romans 12:1-2 (Revised Standard Version)

#296 Perfexpectations Theme: People

Are you disappointed?

Ever been disappointed by another Christian—even your pastor? Maybe you are the problem. Do you feel that pastors—as Christian leaders—ought to be perfect? Did you hear about the man who wanted to have a perfect lawn? One day, he came home and found it filled with dandelions. He couldn't get rid of them. He wrote the Department of Agriculture and asked for help. Their reply was, "We suggest you learn to love them." This approach applies to people—even pastors.

Scripture says: "Love covers over a multitude of sins" (1 Peter 4:8).

Here's Our Prescription:

One of the fruits of the Holy Spirit is love. It is an issue of attitude. Your attitude is the mind's paintbrush. It can color any situation. Don't be part of the problem. Be part of the solution. Don't let human beings—even Christians—disappoint you. Love them. Then you will not disappoint God.

"God is love, and those who live in love live in union with God and God lives in union with them.... We love because God first loved us."
1 John 4:16b, 19 (Good News Translation)

#297 Mr. Grump Theme: People

Do you know Mr. Grump?

Some people occasionally get up on the wrong side of the bed. Others just live there. They are always grumpy. They see life with a cloud over their heads. Their glass is always half empty, never half full. The light they see at the end of the tunnel is a train.

How do you live with Mr. Grump?

Here's Our Prescription:

There are those who fight fire with fire. That is: "Get grumpy right back." The better way to fight fire is with water. Pour on the positive. Lift up the love. Kill that grumpiness with kindness. If Mr. Grump attends your church, there is no better place to start pouring on the positive! It is not really about getting up on the wrong side of the bed, anyway. It is about being on the right side with Jesus.

"Do not let evil defeat you; instead, conquer evil with good."
Romans 12:21 (Good News Translation)

#298 The Best Theme: People

Do you know a *scoundrel*?

I couldn't believe what Bob was saying about George! He cut him down. He complained about his actions. By the time he finished, I was tempted to get on George's case as well. Two weeks later, George was diagnosed with a brain tumor. A week after that, he was dead.

Here's Our Prescription:

As a Christian, always think the best of others. When they hurt or offend you, consider what else might be going on in their lives. Maybe they are under pressure: having family difficulties or health problems. Don't beat them up mentally. Don't drag them through the mud verbally. Give them the benefit of a doubt. Probe what might be the real issue. Pray for them. When it comes to people—expect the best. And tolerate the worst. In prayer, focus on healing the cause—even if you don't know what it is.

> *"This is scary: You can tame a tiger, but you can't tame a tongue—it's never been done. The tongue runs wild, a wanton killer. With our tongues we bless God our Father; with the same tongues we curse the very men and women he made in his image. Curses and blessings out of the same mouth! My friends, this can't go on."*
> *James 3:7-10 (The Message)*

#299 Hope-Full — Theme: People

Where is your hope?

When my wife and I lived in Australia, we learned a phrase about negative people. Aussies call them "no-hopers." No-hopers see the negative side of everything. You might be on fire for a cause. The "no-hopers" around you see themselves as firefighters.

Hopelessness is a distorted mental attitude. It is a focus on the negative. Did you ever wonder about the nightly newscast? There are more positives taking place in life than negatives. There are more people contributing good than those being bad. So, why is the news ninety-five percent negative? Your real source of hope is God! The great news? God sent Jesus to bring hope.

Here's Our Prescription:

If you're a no-hoper—perhaps you need a healed relationship with God. If you are a no-hoper Christian—perhaps you are under attack. There is spiritual power among believers filled with hope. Are you one of them? God hopes so!

"For I know the plans I have for you, says the Lord, plans for welfare and not for evil, to give you a future and a hope."
Jeremiah 29:11 (Revised Standard Version)

#300 Stingy George   Theme: People

Do you live generously?

Meet Stingy George. He gives away one percent of his wealth and thinks it is a big deal. Yet, he is an unhappy person. George is an unhealthy miser. People give him a wide berth everywhere he goes. That makes him worse.

What is your perspective on wealth and generosity? Do you have a positive attitude about giving? No one can explain it, but it is a fact: You can't outgive God.

Here's Our Prescription:

The Bible gives the impression that it is good to give ten percent – of everything God gives you – back to His work, through your church. The word in Scripture is a "tithe" – ten percent. Anything beyond that is an "offering." Do you think you can't afford it? If you want to be spiritually fulfilled, you can't afford not to. It is a leap of faith. Give because you love the Lord. Trust His promises. Giving is not a "money thing" or a "time thing." It is a faith issue – believing He will provide as He promises. The real miracle? Watch the impact it makes on God's work – and you!

"Bring your full tithe to the Temple treasury so there will be ample provisions in my Temple. Test me in this and see if I don't open up heaven itself to you and pour out blessings beyond your wildest dreams."
Malachi 3:10 (The Message)

#301 Oscar the Grouch Theme: People

Do you know Oscar?

Have you ever seen Oscar the Grouch? He is constantly complaining. He sees the negative side of everything. Grouchy people cause pain, discouragement, and frustration. My wife and I were greeters at church. We gave people a warm welcome. It was pouring rain outside. About one out of three came in grumbling about the weather. I just said, "It's not raining in here!" Besides, without rain, you would live in a desert. What do you do when you meet a grouch?

Here's Our Prescription:

Learn to love the grouches in your life. Ask for God's help to overwhelm them with kindness. Express the positive side of their negative comments. Be humble, gentle, and patient. Pray for them. If they start getting you down, ask God for miraculous tolerance. Don't let a grouch steal your Christian joy.

"Be always humble, gentle, and patient. Show your love by being tolerant with one another. Do your best to preserve the unity which the Spirit gives by means of the peace that binds you together."
Ephesians 4:2-3 (Good News Translation)

#302 Percentage Plan Theme: Plan!

Do you have a giving plan?

A young man in high school promised to tithe. He made $100 a week, so he gave $10 back to God through the church offering. He became successful after he finished college and earned $1,000 a week. He thought ten percent—$100—was too much. He asked his pastor how he might keep his promise without giving so much. The pastor prayed: "God, please reduce this man's income back to $100!"

Here's Our Prescription:

At a restaurant, you tip the server based on a percentage. The concept comes from Scripture. God gives us everything and asks for a percentage back for mission and ministry. Percentage giving is God's plan. It doesn't "just" happen. It takes spiritual growth as a disciple. It requires faith in God to supply. You must plan to make it happen. When it does, it releases powerful resources for God's work. The real miracle? It will grow your faith. You can't outgive God.

"This most generous God who gives seed to the farmer that becomes bread for your meals is more than extravagant with you. He gives you something you can then give away, which grows into full-formed lives, robust in God, wealthy in every way, so that you can be generous in every way, producing with us great praise to God."
2 Corinthians 9:10-11 (The Message)

#303 Life Plan Theme: Plan!

Do you have a life plan?

When you plan, you bring the future into the present so you can do something about it now. I asked Bill, "What are you doing today?" His answer was, "I don't have a clue." He was a man without a plan. Guess what? If you fail to plan, you plan to fail.

Here's Our Prescription:

If you don't know God's plan for your entire life, try to figure out His direction for the next decade. If you don't know that, make a plan for this year. If you can't do that, focus on this month. And if that's too much? Just plan today. Start with prayer. Ask God to reveal what He would want you to do. Get out of His way. Let go, and let God. Listen to the nudges He gives. They might come from another person of faith or from a Christian song or Scripture verse. Plan your life. And, with God in charge, live *His* plan for you. Then, you have more than a plan. You have a calling from your Creator!

"We may make our plans, but God has the last word."
Proverbs 16:1 (Good News Translation)

#304 Plan for Significance Theme: Plan!

Do you have a *significance* plan?

I saw this on a sweatshirt: "God put me on earth to accomplish a certain number of things. Right now, I'm so far behind, I'll never die!" What is the most common response to a request for help? "I can't; I'm too busy." If you say that, you need to move from success to significance.

Here's Our Prescription:

Take inventory of your life. List all you do. Then, take a piece of paper and draw a gravestone. Now, put your name on it and your date of birth. Put a dash line and a question mark. Ask yourself, "What words would I like on that stone?" Now focus on what keeps you busy. Will it lead to what you have written? If not, you need a strategy for *significant* change! Don't just count your days. Make your days count!

"Don't waste your time on useless work, mere busywork, the barren pursuits of darkness. Expose these things for the sham they are. It's a scandal when people waste their lives on things they must do in the darkness where no one will see. Rip the cover off those frauds and see how attractive they look in the light of Christ. Wake up from your sleep, climb out of your coffins; Christ will show you the light! So watch your step. Use your head. Make the most of every chance you get. These are desperate times! Don't live carelessly, unthinkingly. Make sure you understand what the Master wants."
Ephesians 5:11-17 (The Message)

#305 Planning for Growth   Theme: Plan!

Do you have a growth plan?

The physician said our son was in the sixty-seventh percentile for height and the fifty-eighth percentile for weight. How do you measure spiritual growth? Perhaps you went to Sunday school as a child. Maybe you joined a church. How would you score your SQ—spiritual quotient?

Former UCLA coach John Wooden said, "It's what you learn after you know it all that counts." Do you have a plan to grow spiritually?

Here's Our Prescription:

Direct a portion of your time for your spiritual growth. Design half of that for personal growth. Direct the other half to develop your gifts and skills to grow God's Kingdom. Learn to be a missionary to your community. Ask God to grow you spiritually—beyond yourself, for others. Get involved in your city and your nation for Christ. That is spiritual maturity.

"To win the contest you must deny yourselves many things that would keep you from doing your best....We do it for a heavenly reward that never disappears."
1 Corinthians 9:25 (The Living Bible)

#306 Planning for Eternity Theme: Plan!

Do you have an eternal worldview?

Martin Luther was asked, "What would you do if you knew Jesus was coming back tomorrow?" He said, "I'd plant a tree!" What was he saying? On your last day, you shouldn't be doing anything differently. Live each day like you are on the edge of eternity. One day, you will be right!

Here's Our Prescription:

Don't put off spiritual matters. You don't know when your time will end! If you need to get back to God—do it now. If you need to reconcile a relationship—do it now. If you need to share your faith with someone—do it now. If you need to serve God at your church—do it now. If you think you should plant a tree—do it now. Every day, you live your life on the edge of eternity.

"Watch out, then, because you do not know what day your Lord will come…. So then, you also must always be ready, because the Son of Man will come at an hour when you are not expecting him."
Matthew 24:42, 44 (Good News Translation)

#307 Porcupines Theme: Plan!

Has someone hurt you?

Chuck Swindoll once said that Christians are like a pack of porcupines on a cold night. The cold drives us together in a huddle to keep warm. But the closer we get, the more our "quills" jab each other. That forces us apart. Then, we get cold again and huddle. You have likely experienced tension. Christians come together to do God's work. However, sometimes we hurt each other with our words and actions. Even as Christ-followers, we occasionally "poke" one another. Does that discourage you?

Here's Our Prescription:

Ask for God's power and grace to love others—no matter how they treat you. Perhaps you heard that you should "love God and trust people." Yet, how can you *trust* imperfect people? The Bible says, "*Trust* God and love people." From that perspective, you can forgive them. If you live under the grace of God, focus on God's approach. Don't be a porcupine out in the cold! Warm up to God's plan: Trust God and love people.

"God is my savior; I will trust him and not be afraid. The Lord gives me power and strength; he is my savior. As fresh water brings joy to the thirsty, so God's people rejoice when he saves them."
Isaiah 12:2-3 (Good News Translation)

#308 Ageless Plans Theme: Plan!

Will you live until you die?

Your attitude is more important than your age. Consider my friend Sid. At eighty-nine, he was one of the "youngest" servants of God I ever met. Whit Hobbs wrote, "Success is waking up in the morning, whoever you are, wherever you are, however old or young, and bounding out of bed because there's something out there you love to do, you believe in, you're good at—something bigger than you are, and you can hardly wait to get at it again today." What are you eager to do today?

Here's Our Prescription:

Don't look at the negative side of aging. It won't make you younger. It won't energize you, either. Develop a lifelong plan of service to God. Serving God energizes. Why? You work for the King of the universe! I met a woman from the US in northwestern Thailand. Her husband had died. At age seventy, she became a missionary! Commit to God's work. You will jump out of bed faster. Why? Your Creator energizes you—for life!

"Acknowledge that the Lord is God. He made us, and we belong to him; we are his people, we are his flock.... The Lord is good; his love is eternal and his faithfulness lasts forever."
Psalm 100:3, 5 (Good News Translation)

#309 Sensitize! Theme: Posture

How do you act around others?

Whether at work or school or among neighbors, you are likely among some unbelievers. Many do not have a relationship with the Lord. They are unaware they need Him. How can you help without being pushy, arrogant, or preachy?

Here's Our Prescription:

Be sensitive! You have to earn the right to be heard. How? Listen to their thoughts and views. Develop a receptive environment by building a relationship. Once you have earned trust, share your own story about what Jesus has done in your life. Talk about your struggles. Be honest about your doubts. However, give God credit for getting you through. Show genuine love to others. Why? God has demonstrated His love for you. You are likely the most effective witness for Jesus because you have the relationship. God's Kingdom grows best through genuine friendships.

"Now that I've put you on a hilltop, on a light stand – shine! Keep open house; be generous with your lives. By opening up to others, you'll prompt people to open up with God, this generous Father in heaven."
Matthew 5:15-16 (The Message)

#310 Bridges That Connect Theme: Posture

Are you a bridge builder?

Years ago, if you invited someone to church, they would likely respond. Today, the world is much different. Many have no church background. They don't consider church relevant. They fear that all the church wants is their money. The best way to reach people today is to follow the approach used by missionaries: Make divine contact.

Here's Our Prescription:

Build a bridge by meeting needs. Often, the greatest need is genuine friendship. Consider those in your circle of influence: friends, relatives, neighbors, colleagues at work, or friends at school. What needs do they have? Identify the issues you can address. In the context of those bridges, share how Jesus has impacted your life. Build authentic relationships. Sharing the good news is like electricity: It flows best where there is good contact. Let your divine contact be the bridge that brings the light of Christ to your relationships!

"...And every day the Lord added to their group those who were being saved."
Acts 2:47 (Good News Translation)

#311 Re-New Theme: Posture

Do you have a temperature?

God has called us to be thermostats, not thermometers. Thermometers simply record the temperature. However, thermostats set the temperature. Are you on fire for God? Do you pray God will use you to ignite spiritual renewal?

In my prayer life, I pray for revival, beginning with me. Will you fire up your spiritual life?

Here's Our Prescription:

Get into God's Word regularly. Don't just read it academically. Let God speak to you deeply. Catch the warmth of a personal touch from Jesus. Get close to other Christians who fan your flames. Connect with those who encourage you to grow spiritually and share your faith courageously. Pray for opportunities to share your faith. Ask God to bring a revival, beginning with you.

"Then their eyes were opened and they recognized him [Jesus], but he disappeared from their sight. They said to each other, 'Wasn't it like a fire burning in us when he talked to us on the road and explained the Scriptures to us?'"
Luke 24:31-32 (Good News Translation)

#312 Taking the Marbles Theme: Posture

Are you looking for perfection?

When the going gets tough, some people leave their church! Think of Noah's ark with all those animals. Can you imagine what it smelled like after two weeks? However, nobody got off the boat!

Every church experiences rough times. If you jump ship when there is a problem, you could spend your life hopping from one congregation to another. There is a perfect church—but it is not on *this* earth. Your church is a family. Every family has challenges. Yet, if there is any family that can rise above difficulties, it should be the church.

Here's Our Prescription:

When the going gets tough, don't say, "I'm going to take my marbles and leave." Stay. Exercise your faith, and be part of the solution! Give God the opportunity to strengthen you, even as you are tested by the fire of difficulties. Your church is not a country club for perfect people, but a hospital for forgiven sinners.

"My dear friends, stand firm and don't be shaken.
Always keep busy working for the Lord. You know
that everything you do for him is worthwhile."
1 Corinthians 15:58 (Contemporary English Version)

#313 Civility　　Theme: Posture

Who is in charge?

When you drive, do you watch the speed limit? Or, do you look for a parked police car—to avoid a speeding ticket? What do you call that? Honestly, it is a rebellion against authority.

"Civility" means "respect." When you respect others, you are "civilized." In our imperfect world, there are many who show little respect for law enforcement, teachers, pastors, the government, even God.

Here's Our Prescription:

Whether it be the right to life, obedience to the speed limit, sending appropriate emails, respect for parents, a willingness to follow church leaders, honoring your pastors, or submission to God's Word—humbly pray, "Lord, by your strength, help me do better." It is God plan, and it works. You can make this a better world—with God's help.

"...whoever rebels against the authority is rebelling against what God has instituted, and those who do so will bring judgment on themselves."
Romans 13:2 (New International Version)

#314 The Packaging Theme: Posture

What is *in* the package?

The Pharisees wanted to hold onto the old style and tradition. Jesus said truth doesn't change, but it comes in new packages. The birth of Jesus was God in a new package. The challenge? People tend to identify the packaging as "sacred." Jesus—the content—never changes. The truth is forever. Everything else changes. For some Christians, it appears easier to change biblical truth than it is to replace the worn-out carpet!

Have you experienced biblical faith in new packaging?

Here's Our Prescription:

Ask God to help you be open to new styles of worship songs, instruments, and translations of Scripture. Packaging changes from age to age. It *must* change to be relevant. However, truth must remain the same. When you catch that concept, you will reach new generations. The content can't change. The containers must change.

"Nor does anyone pour new wine into used wineskins, for the skins will burst, the wine will pour out, and the skins will be ruined. Instead, new wine is poured into fresh wineskins, and both will keep in good condition."
Matthew 9:17 (Good News Translation)

#315 Cardiac Concrete Theme: Posture

Does your heart ever grow hard?

An old farmer sold his mule, Marvin, to his friend, Larry. But later, Larry couldn't get Marvin to move. Larry called the farmer to come and help. The farmer took a big board and hit Marvin over the head. Then he moved! Larry remarked, "You could have killed him!" The old farmer said, "No, in order to get Marvin moving, first you have to get his attention!"

Most Christians can remember a time when God got their attention at a whole new level. God won't hit you over the head with a board. However, sometimes He will allow you to be challenged. Is God trying to get your attention?

Here's Our Prescription:

If you suffer from being stubborn, it may be time to get down on your knees. Humble yourself before God. Speak to the Lord in prayer. Ask Him to take first place in your life. Get into your Bible. Submit yourself to His truth. A reality hit with humility might seem painful. Yet, sometimes, God wants to get your attention.

"Sometimes it takes a painful experience to make us change our ways."
Proverbs 20:30 (Good News Translation)

#316 Risky Love Theme: Risk

Have you been drafted?

Christ-followers have marching orders: "Go and make disciples." You have been called to share God's love, feed the hungry, heal the sick, help the poor, fight for justice, and point people to Jesus. It is a call to get off the cruise ship and onto the battleship.

God is looking for an army, not an audience: not a force armed with guns and bullets. He wants those who share His love. It is a different kind of army—one that moves forward on its knees. With God's presence, you are powerful.

Here's Our Prescription:

Ask God to mobilize you for action. You will become a vital part of God's army of love. As a soldier for God, you are called to capture new territory, take more ground, and change our world—one person at a time. Are you focused on God's mission? It isn't risky, but powerful! You don't shoot to kill, but love to save.

"You're familiar with the old written law, 'Love your friend,' and its unwritten companion, 'Hate your enemy.' In a word, what I'm saying is, Grow up. You're kingdom subjects. Now live like it. Live out your God-created identity. Live generously and graciously toward others, the way God lives toward you."

Matthew 5:43, 48 (The Message)

#317 Outhouse Theme: Risk

Can you imagine a church without walls?

Christianity is a lot like manure. Pile it up, and it stinks up the neighborhood. Spread it around, and it enriches the world. If the love of Jesus isn't spread, it's dead. You can be dead right. Scholars call it "dead orthodoxy": right beliefs, but no mission.

If every Christian would win one other person to Christ in the next calendar year, the multiplication of believers would far surpass any spiritual movement in history. This is nothing revolutionary. It has been the same directive from Jesus for the last two thousand years. Are you taking your faith beyond the walls of your church?

Here's Our Prescription:

Move beyond your church world. Get Jesus into your neighborhood, your community, your workplace, your school. Don't let your church insulate you. Motivate your church to mobilize a movement. Don't let your faith isolate you from outsiders, but let it equip you to reach them. As a Christ-follower, you have a purpose. Spread the love!

"You, LORD, give perfect peace to those who keep their purpose firm and put their trust in you."
Isaiah 26:3 (Good News Translation)

#318 Midlife Calling   Theme: Risk

Are you in crisis mode?

Meet Mike. He is a successful businessman who started a plastics company. However, God was tugging at his heart for years. Eventually, he sold his company. Mike made a career change. He started working for his church.

What about you? Is God calling you beyond your career to serve Him? This is occurring all over the world. Your friends might call it a midlife crisis. God calls it a midlife *calling*.

Here's Our Prescription:

If God is moving you, talk to a Christian career counselor. Look at the thousands of ways you can work for Jesus. Is it risky? Sure! Just remember: The Christian God calls to service is the one who makes the right move, at the right time, with the right motive, for the right cause. If you get the call, answer it. Trust God—it could be the best move you ever make.

"Those who trust in the Lord are steady as Mount Zion, unmoved by any circumstance."
Psalm 125:1 (The Living Bible)

#319 Recipe for Reciprocity Theme: Risk

Are you investing wisely?

Did you ever hear someone say, "We can't afford that"? Have you said it yourself? Where is your faith? Faith says, "If impossible is the only obstacle, it can be done." Faith takes you where reason can't go. You can count the seeds in an apple, but you can't count the apples in a seed. Faith is that seed in God's hand.

The Bible says you should give financially to God's work as He has provided for you. It is about returning a portion, a percentage, off the top.

Here's Our Prescription:

When you receive income, the first part goes to God. Even if you receive a gift, some goes to God. This is the recipe for reciprocity. God has given you gifts—special abilities. Whatever God provides, give back a portion. You are reinvesting in God's work, a sure thing! The miracle? You can't outgive God when you show God how much He matters to you. Show God your heart.

"...store up riches for yourselves in heaven, where moths and rust cannot destroy, and robbers cannot break in and steal. For your heart will always be where your riches are."
Matthew 6:20-21 (Good News Translation)

#320 Inviting Friends to Meet God

Theme: Risk

Are you extending an invitation?

Many years ago, I was telling my friend, Ray, about how much our son, Jonathan, enjoyed basketball. Ray said he had season tickets for the Chicago Bulls. He offered me tickets to take my son. It was an unforgettable experience!

It was a treat to see Michael Jordan play before he retired. However, there is no comparison to experiencing the living God. Are you connected to Jesus? Do you connect others to Him?

Here's Our Prescription:

Most of your unchurched friends would join you for an informal discussion about faith if you simply invited them. Make a list of people you know who are not believers. Pray for them. Watch for the right time. Start with an invitation to dinner. Share what your faith in Jesus has done for you. Just tell your story of faith. Let your spiritual light shine.

"'If I make you light-bearers, you don't think I'm going to hide you under a bucket, do you? I'm putting you on a light stand.'"
Matthew 5:15 (The Message)

#321 Rejection — Theme: Risk

Are you paralyzed by fear?

I was talking to my friend Don one day and asked if his neighbor is a person of faith. He said, "I've lived next to him most of my life. I don't think he has ever been to church." "Did you ever invite him?" I asked. "Yeah, I did once. He just wasn't interested." I asked, "When was that?" "Oh, probably twenty years ago," he said.

Don was rejected once. So, he never asked his neighbor again. Do you ever think about telling others about Jesus or sharing your story of faith?

Here's Our Prescription:

Don't give up because someone wasn't interested. People change. They can become more receptive. How? Through the challenges of life. Remember, God's Spirit speaks through you. Keep this perspective: If they are not interested, it is not you they are rejecting. It is God. Don't let your fear paralyze what God wants to do through you!

"The one who listens to you, listens to me. The one who rejects you, rejects me. And rejecting me is the same as rejecting God, who sent me."
Luke 10:16 (The Message)

#322 Cutting Edge **Theme: Risk**

Are you on the edge?

A man fell off a cliff. On the way down, he grabbed a root. He looked up to heaven and said, "Oh, God, help me." To his surprise, a voice responded: "I will save you. Just let go." The man thought for a moment, looked to heaven, and said, "Is there anybody else I can talk to up there?"

There is no one else! Faith includes a willingness to risk. It is called a step of faith. It is trusting God for the impossible. Where is God calling you? What is God calling you to do?

Here's Our Prescription:

If you are not living on the edge, you are taking up too much room! Is it time for you to grow in your faith? Do you need to take a leap of faith? You can't discover new oceans unless you have the courage to lose sight of the shore. Pray for courage! Let go, and let God!

"...we fix our attention, not on things that are seen, but on things that are unseen."
2 Corinthians 4:18a (Good News Translation)

#323 Agendas   Theme: Conflict

Are you a person who has an agenda?

The sergeant said, "After you jump, count to ten. Pull the rip cord. If that chute doesn't open, pull the second rip cord. When you land, take the truck back to the base." The young soldier jumped, pulled the rip cord, and the chute didn't open! He pulled the second rip cord, and nothing happened. "Oh, great," he complained, "I bet the truck won't be there, either!"

Are you a planner? Do you make plans: for your family, your career, and your vacation? Do you have a plan for your spiritual life? Are your plans in line with God's plan? They are called spiritual agendas. They lead to a leap of faith.

Here's Our Prescription:

Spend time thinking—and praying—about what God wants for you: not necessarily what you want. Humbly submit your agenda to God. Ask: "Is my agenda God's plan?" How do you know God's plans? Read the manual. It is called the Bible. Take a leap of faith. Discover God's hope for you. Even when you fall, He will be there for you.

"This is God's Word on the subject.... 'I know what I'm doing. I have it all planned out—plans to take care of you, not abandon you, plans to give you the future you hope for.'"
Jeremiah 29:10a, 11 (The Message)

#324 Loudspeaker   Theme: Conflict

Are you living out loud?

Sean works for a marketing group. He has noticed lately that work is taking him in a direction against his Christian values. He feels caught between his conscience and keeping his job. Sean feels like he is between a rock and a hard place.

Do you find yourself in situations like that? Perhaps it is with a group of friends where the language has become offensive. Maybe you have a relative cheating on her taxes. Maybe it is a friend who is into drugs. What do you do?

Here's Our Prescription:

Speak up; speak out. In love, share from your heart. The Bible says, "Speak the truth in a spirit of love." Be honest: You are uncomfortable because you care. Then share the benefits of living with integrity. Talk about how God helps you. Of course you feel like you are between a rock and a hard place. Jesus gets that. He has been there: on a cross, so you don't have to be, ever. He will give you strength to speak out in love.

"For the Spirit that God has given us does not make us timid; instead, his Spirit fills us with power, love, and self-control."
2 Timothy 1:7 (Good News Translation)

#325 Lens Correction Theme: Conflict

Do you wear glasses or contacts?

When our son played football in high school, we would practice throwing and catching the ball. This is what we discovered: You can't catch what you don't see coming. We learned that he needed a lens correction. He got contacts!

God's Word—Scripture—says a lot about our weaknesses. Yet, it has much more to say about forgiveness, restoration, and new life. When you discover the Ruler of the universe loves you, forgives you, and empowers you—it is a major lens correction.

Here's Our Prescription:

If you were the only person on Earth, Jesus would have died for you. That is your lens for yourself and as you look at others. God's mission is to empower us to win the world for Jesus Christ! It is not a game. Jesus demonstrated that each person has value. That lens correction changes everything: who we are, what we do, and who we become.

"...be concerned above everything else with the Kingdom of God and with what he requires of you, and he will provide you with all these other things."
Matthew 6:33 (Good News Translation)

#326 Grumbling Theme: Conflict

Are you grumbling?

Have you heard the phrase, "If it's not broken, don't fix it"? We live in a world that is constantly changing. Does that make you uncomfortable? Sometimes change is necessary. Most innovations in churches are initiated by those who mean well. There are two different types of change in the realm of faith. The content—Scripture—must never change. The Bible is sacred. But the strategies? They change to be effective. When methods change, do you grumble?

Here's Our Prescription:

Don't become upset about a strategic change at your church. Talk with others who can help you understand. Your grumbling doesn't help your attitude, and it doesn't inspire others. Pray and read Scripture. Learn about God's will—what God wants. And if you see God's hand in it, get behind the change. Wouldn't your church thrive with an atmosphere like that?

"Stephen, a man blessed by God ... was opposed by some men who were members of the synagogue.... 'We heard him say that this Jesus of Nazareth will...change all the customs....' 'How stubborn you are!' Stephen went on to say. 'How heathen your hearts, how deaf you are to God's message!'"
Acts 6:8-9, 14; 7:51 (Good News Translation)

#327 Discomfort — Theme: Conflict

Are you uncomfortable with change?

Mark Twain said, "The only person who likes change is a baby with a wet diaper." Time spent complaining about change is time lost sharing it. It is amazing how many Christians struggle with change. Christ-followers know more about change than anyone. Repentance is change. Forgiveness is transformational! The Bible says we change from old to new, from death to life. Yet, many seasoned Christians resist change. Do you?

Here's Our Prescription:

God is more interested in your character than your comfort. Ask yourself: Are you changing religion or changing faith? Religion is style, the programs that help you express your faith. Faith is the content, truths that never change. Truths are the principles of faith. Programs are many; principles are few. Programs always change; principles never do.

"Let there be real harmony so that there won't be splits in the church. I plead with you to be of one mind, united in thought and purpose."
1 Corinthians 1:10b (The Living Bible)

#328 Uptight Insight Theme: Conflict

Are you feeling uptight?

Ever been frustrated about some issue at church? What do you do about feelings and frustrations? Tension often occurs when you work with others. However, tension isn't always bad. You were born out of tension—your mother's labor pains!

Here's Our Prescription:

Not all frustrations are problems. Some may be God's way to give you new insight—lead you to a new faith level. Don't ever quit. Quitting is a permanent solution to a temporary challenge. Most people who succeed in the face of seemingly impossible conditions are those who don't know how to quit. In some churches, the problems stay, and the people leave. In other churches, the people stay, and the problems leave. What will you do?

"From the depths of my despair I call to you, Lord. Hear my cry, O Lord; listen to my call for help! If you kept a record of our sins, who could escape being condemned?"
Psalm 130:1-3 (Good News Translation)

#329 Conflicting Expectations? Theme: Conflict

Has someone let you down?

Rob was frustrated with Chris. This was the third week in a row he hadn't set up the room properly for Bible class. So, Rob confronted him. Chris protested, saying that Rob had never shown him how to do it. They talked and worked it out. The word "conflict" means "to strike together." A war is a conflict. So is an emotional disturbance with an inability to reconcile.

Do Christians have conflicts? Yes! Christians aren't perfect—just forgiven.

Here's Our Prescription:

Trust God. You will never be disappointed. The next time you are in conflict with someone, use Scripture as your guide. Start with prayer. Ask God to use you to spread light, not heat. Then, go to the person and work it out—privately. Always remember, if you think you are perfect, check your pulse! If you are alive, you are not perfect—yet. You are forgiven—to be forgiving.

"If your brother sins against you, go to him and show him his fault. But do it privately, just between yourselves. If he listens to you, you have won your brother back."
Matthew 18:15 (Good News Translation)

#330 Thanksgiving for Growth

Theme: Thanksgiving

Is your family growing?

The preacher waded into the river to baptize a man whose life had been very sinful. The preacher announced to him, "Your sins have been washed away." The man looked at the water and said, "God, have mercy on all those fish."

It is miraculous—the way God transforms lives! Every day, Jesus leads people to Himself. The other miracle? He uses people just like you to do it!

Here's Our Prescription:

Do you thank God for the growth of the Christian movement? Do you celebrate when someone becomes a believer? Will you thank God for guests who visit your church? Do you praise Him when someone is baptized or when a new family joins your church? If your church is growing, thank God. Celebrate the grace of God, and encourage other Christians to do the same.

"...I tell you, the angels of God rejoice over one sinner who repents."
Luke 15:10 (Good News Translation)

#331 Gratitude

Theme: Thanksgiving

Are you grateful?

It is said that the Spirit of Christ is the spirit of missions. The closer you get to Jesus, the more mission-minded you become. As one missionary put it, "If Jesus Christ is God and died for me, then no sacrifice can be too great for me to make for Him."

Are you grateful that God has forgiven you in Jesus Christ? Do you appreciate the sure hope of salvation? Join the mission. It is one of the best ways to celebrate your faith!

Here's Our Prescription:

If you knew the cure for cancer, would you keep it a secret? God's love and forgiveness are even greater! So, get your personal mission started. How? Pray for those you know who are without faith. Focus on those in your social network. They are in your phone directory. You carry them around every day. Pray for the opportunity to share God's love. Watch for those going through difficulties. Pray with them. In a spirit of gratitude, reach out!

"Make it as clear as you can to all you meet that you're on their side, working with them and not against them. Help them see that the Master is about to arrive. He could show up any minute!"
Philippians 4:5 (The Message)

#332 Gratuation

Theme: Thanksgiving

Are you grateful for your church?

Remember the ten lepers? All were healed. Only one came back to say, "Thanks." Jesus wondered, "Where are the other nine?" Does He wonder where you are ninety percent of the time? Nine times out of ten, most people forget to be grateful. Change that, beginning with yourself.

Here's Our Prescription:

Thank your pastor at least once every month—and the leaders of your church. Thank those who lead worship. Thank those who serve as ushers, Sunday school teachers, and Vacation Bible School teachers. Thank the office help and custodians. Thank those who work in hospitality. Thank those who serve the poor. Make thanksgiving a year-round lifestyle. Most of all, thank God for Jesus—every day. Grow in thanksgiving—and graduate to gratitude!

"Pray diligently. Stay alert, with your eyes wide open in gratitude."
Colossians 4:2 (The Message)

#333 Gratuanity

Theme: Thanksgiving

Are you thankful?

The doctor said, "Bill, if you have anything important to do with your right hand, you'd better do it now. You have gangrene, and we must amputate immediately." Bill folded his hands and thanked God. Do you ever think of all that your church has done for you? What about that Sunday school teacher when you were a kid? The minister when your dad died? The sermon that spoke right to your personal challenge? What about those who treat you like family?

If you are a member of a church, you have been blessed.

Here's Our Prescription:

To be blessed is to become supernaturally happy. List all the ways God has blessed you through your church. Use your list as a thanksgiving prayer guide. Share it with your family and friends. Update it once every six months. Experience what it means to discover an attitude of gratitude. Celebrate gratitude for your faith, for Jesus. Make your Christianity gratuanity!

"Every time I think of you, I give thanks to my God."
Philippians 1:3 (New Living Translation)

#334 Gratigram

Theme: Thanksgiving

Did I hear you say, "Thank you"?

Cicero said, "Gratitude is not only the greatest of virtues, but the parent of the others." Christians thank God for His blessings. That includes people around us who are kind and gracious, those who serve others. It is so important to show thanks. If you are a parent, how hard did you work to remind your kids to say, "Thanks"? At our house, I believe we said it more than a thousand times. Now, our kids are adults. Guess what? It worked!

Here's Our Prescription:

Send a text. Call it a "gratigram." Write a note or card with a message—a special way to say, "Thanks." Get a stack of thank-you notes. Whenever you appreciate some kindness, share a verbal thank you. Or, send an email—whatever works for you. Just do it. Make it a life habit. Why? It is healthy to show appreciation. It encourages those who are kind. What if everyone sent one gratigram every day? You could start a revolution—of kindness!

"...ever since I heard about your faith in the Lord Jesus and your love for all God's people, I have not stopped giving thanks for you, remembering you in my prayers."
Ephesians 1:15-16 (New International Version)

#335 Grat-attitude

Theme: Thanksgiving

Do you thank God—often?

Most people find it easier to ask God for something than to thank Him. There is the story about a pastor who served a little church in a fishing village. His year-end statistics showed nine people missing at sea. But the people in the congregation didn't know of anyone who was lost. So, they asked what he meant. He explained: "Eleven people asked me to pray for family members going out to sea, but only two asked me to pray for thanks when they returned. So, I assumed the other nine had been lost." It was a little "over the top," but they got the message!

Here's Our Prescription:

Put a note on your dresser, the refrigerator, your iPad or tablet, or the bathroom mirror. Write the words: "Think thanks." Use it as a reminder to approach God every day with an attitude of gratitude. No matter what your circumstances, you will discover: You can thank God for so much!

"I will praise you, LORD, with all my heart; I will tell of all the wonderful things you have done."
Psalm 9:1 (Good News Translation)

#336 For Granted

Theme: Thanksgiving

What do you take for granted?

One day, the great preacher Charles Spurgeon was robbed. He told his wife he was thankful. Surprised, she asked why. "I'm thankful the robber took my money, not my life. I'm thankful I left most of my money at home. And, I'm thankful to God I was not the robber."

How often we take life for granted!

Here's Our Prescription:

Make a list of what you take for granted. Put that list somewhere as a reminder to thank God. Note: Did you, like Spurgeon, thank God for what you are *not*? What dangers you missed? The temptations you avoided? After two weeks, list what you could be doing to share your blessings with others. Do this often. You will take less for granted! If you need a visual reminder, try this: Focus on the doughnut, not the hole.

"If you search for good, you will find favor; but if you search for evil, it will find you!"
Proverbs 11:27 (New Living Translation)

#337 The Lonely Crowd

Theme: Connection

Do you feel lonely?

Why is God's "Plan A" that people enter this world in a family—and not alone? Why would Scripture say, "Where two or more are gathered in (Jesus') name, He is present" (Matthew 18:20)? We all need other people. Not just anyone, however. Life is all about relationships. Ever been lonely in a crowd? You can be surrounded by people, yet feel all alone.

Jesus said, when you show love to others, it demonstrates love for Him.

Here's Our Prescription:

Reorganize your hectic schedule so you can adopt a friend who has no one. Dedicate a slice of your life to someone in a nursing home, in jail, or at the rescue mission. Be a mentor for a kid. Share your time, your hope, your friendship, and your love. Share your faith—your best friend, Jesus. Connect with the unconnected. Neither of you will feel alone.

"For the whole law can be summed up in this one command: 'Love your neighbor as yourself.'"
Galatians 5:14 (New Living Translation)

#338 Friendly Sailing

Theme: Connection

Are you a friend?

Do you know the way to discover how many friends you have? Rent a condo at the beach. Another approach is to look around your church. Friendship is the glue that holds Christians together. The Bible's word for it is "fellowship." One of the ancient symbols for the church is a ship—perhaps influenced by Noah's ark. A friendly church is a friend-*ship*, a fellow-*ship*. You are an important part of the member-*ship*. Why? Relation-*ships* change a *cold* organization into a *warm* family.

You can be an icebreaker!

Here's Our Prescription:

Smile. Connect with others. Become a friendly greeter. Be positive and optimistic. Make it a point to encourage five people every time you worship. One person can be a spark that lights a fire that warms a church. You can be that spark. Relation-*ships* are contagious. They can reorganize a rigid bureaucracy to become a caring family. So, get on board God's friend-*ship*.

"They spent their time in learning from the apostles, taking part in the fellowship, and sharing in the fellowship meals and the prayers."
Acts 2:42 (Good News Translation)

#339 Eternal Friendship

Theme: Connection

Are you an influencer?

Everyone influences others. What you say and do shapes those around you: for good or bad. It is an awesome responsibility. The power of personal influence is amazing. And, God wants you to use it—for the eternal benefit of others.

Here's Our Prescription:

List those who are in your "circle of influence." Make categories for friends, relatives, neighbors, and those at work or school. Put the four categories in the four corners of a piece of paper. Draw a circle in the middle, and put your name in the circle. Draw lines to each of the categories. This is your primary "sphere of influence." It is a gift from God. Make it your prayer list. Look for opportunities to share Jesus with those who don't yet know Him. If God moves them to faith through you, the friendship is eternal!

"This is the very best way to love. Put your life on the line for your friends."
John 15:13 (The Message)

#340 Fellowship Ed

Theme: Connection

Have you stopped growing?

Did you attend Sunday school as a kid? Did you quit spiritual growth when you got older? The devil doesn't fear a Bible with dust on it. However, he is petrified when the pages are worn. Christian faith is a lifelong growth experience. Most preachers would agree: A weekly sermon is never enough. What is the best way to grow more in your faith? Get together with other Christians who want to increase their faith.

Here's Our Prescription:

Join an adult Sunday school class at your church. Or, start a Bible study fellowship in your home. You could also meet at a coffee shop and take your spiritual growth public. Invite others to join you. No healthy person eats food only on Sundays. Nourish your faith and fellowship. Get stronger spiritually. You will discover biblical health at a whole new level.

"...we must thank God at all times for you. It is right for us to do so, because your faith is growing so much and the love each of you has for the others is becoming greater."

2 Thessalonians 1:3 (Good News Translation)

#341 Spiritual Navel-Gazing Theme: Connection

Are you navel-gazing?

Have you ever seen the holy huddle before worship? Christians gather around in a circle with their friends—their backs to the outside. For face-to-face contact, a guest would have to squeeze through their legs and pop up in the middle. Most visitors aren't going to do that! Those Christians are practicing a "friendly church"—to each other!

What is the issue? It is spiritual navel-gazing. It results from being so heavenly minded you are no earthly good. You can break the holy huddle.

Here's Our Prescription:

At church, greet your friends, and move on. Look for strangers. Welcome those who are all alone. Go out of your way for those who are new. Be a greeter at the door. Become a greeter in the parking lot. Or, become an "undercover" greeter. Start a ministry of friendly greeting. Extend fellowship, connect with others, and get beyond religious navel-gazing!

"Welcome one another, therefore, as Christ has welcomed you, for the glory of God."
Romans 15:7 (Revised Standard Version)

#342 Fly Right

Theme: Connection

Are you flying solo?

A young Air Force pilot was separated from the jets in formation. The weather deteriorated. His plane ran low on fuel. Without the other jets, he might never find the base on his own. With minutes to spare, the jets found the young pilot and guided him safely to the ground. Later he said, "I realized that staying with my group meant more than anything in the world!" What about you? You may face fear, tragedy, anxiety, or pain. But no one ever said you had to do it alone.

Here's Our Prescription:

Join a small group of Christians. Like the pilot, connect with those who will help guide you through the obstacles of life. A small group of fellow believers can provide encouragement and prayer support. Don't wait until you are near empty and crashing. Link up with fellow believers now, and forge friendships that last. Help guide one another to your eternal home.

"Christ is like a single body, which has many parts; it is still one body, even though it is made up of different parts.... If one part of the body suffers, all the other parts suffer with it; if one part is praised, all the other parts share its happiness."
1 Corinthians 12:12, 26 (Good News Translation)

#343 Building Up

Theme: Connection

Are you building up anyone?

Eleanor is frustrated. Life hasn't been going well—at work, with her daughter, or as Sunday school superintendent at church. The bottom line: She's discouraged! She needs encouragement! In the Bible, it is called building up one another. It occurs when another Christian comes along to help.

Walt Kallestad says, "I am convinced that God's toughest job is making us believe we are valuable. And God recruits us to help Him in building up one another."

Here's Our Prescription:

Watch for those who are discouraged. Pray for them. Offer to pray with them. Take responsibility to build them up. Ask God for the courage to encourage. Become the champion for restoration. Help others know they are valuable—to you, to God. Those you help will become courageous and leave discouragement behind.

> *"So speak encouraging words to one another. Build up hope so you'll all be together in this, no one left out, no one left behind."*
> *1 Thessalonians 5:11 (The Message)*

#344 Age

Theme: Stewardship

What is your age?

The little boy asked his grandfather if he was with Noah on the ark. His grandpa said, "No." The little boy asked, "Then why didn't you drown?" No matter how old you are, age is relative. I've seen "young" people in their nineties and "old" people at eighteen. To some extent, "age" includes attitude.

So, do you go through life as a young person wishing you were older, or as an old person wanting to be younger?

Here's Our Prescription:

Thank God for your season of life right now. Enjoy every season you experience. Put life into perspective. Consider this: Add twenty-five years to your age. Will you be alive? What about one hundred years? Will you be remembered? Focus on managing your life well—in all of your seasons. Learn from yesterday; live for today; plan for tomorrow. And with faith in Jesus, get excited about eternity. It will be your best season of all!

"The LORD is my light and my salvation; whom shall I fear? The LORD is the stronghold of my life; of whom shall I be afraid?"
Psalm 27:1 (Revised Standard Version)

#345 Timely Excuses

Theme: Stewardship

What is your excuse?

Perhaps you have been asked to help at church. What is your reaction? The most common response? "I don't have time." Do you seriously consider *how* you decide if you will get involved? How do you choose "yes" or "no"?

You have the same amount of time as everyone. No one gets twenty-five hours in a day. Do you fall into the trap: "I'm too busy"? It is important to think clearly about the criteria you use to decide.

Here's Our Prescription:

Examine whether you use time wisely. Don't make excuses. Think about reasons—why you should be involved, or why you shouldn't. Ask, "Is it a worthy cause? Does it fit my gifts? Does God want me to do it? What level of impact will it make?" The next time you are asked to serve, don't respond with a cliché. Make your first response, "I'll pray about it!" Then, *really* pray about it.

"Try to learn what pleases the Lord. Have nothing to do with the worthless things that people do…."
Ephesians 5:10-11 (Good News Translation)

#346 Measuring Time

Theme: Stewardship

Are you efficient?

Cathy is a frenzied mom. When her day at work ends, she is at the school minutes later. She drops one kid off at soccer and the other at ballet. The next hour is a race through the grocery store, then it's home to cook dinner and back to pick up the kids.

Ever feel like you can't jam in anything else?

Here's Our Prescription:

Maybe you shouldn't try! Or, perhaps you should delete something. At the other extreme, look at your busy life differently. What can you accomplish during that time with the kids in the car? Find out what's going on in their lives. Look for double value in every experience. Don't simply focus on being *efficient*—getting it done. Practice *effective* life management—doing it with purpose. If you've got a hectic life, make the most of it—for you, for your family, and for God. Ask the Lord for guidance, balance, and endurance.

"May the Master take you by the hand and lead you along the path of God's love and Christ's endurance."
2 Thessalonians 3:5 (The Message)

#347 Invest in the Best

Theme: Stewardship

How do you invest?

Do you know how they catch a monkey in Brazil? They put a glass jar with a narrow neck at the bottom of a tree. They place bananas in the jar. The jar is chained to the tree. The monkey grabs the banana, but can't get its hand out as long as it holds onto the banana. Unwilling to let go, the monkey ends up in a zoo!

Are you trapped because you are "hanging on to a banana"?

Here's Our Prescription:

God doesn't want *everything* you have. In fact, He lets you keep the biggest portion: of your time, energy, and money. Just don't overlook His portion. Look at it as a percentage. Start with a percent. Then aim for ten percent. Grow to fifteen percent. Mature to an even greater amount. It is a spiritual mystery: You can't outgive God. It is a strategy with God's guaranteed return on investment. Let go. Allow God to grow your generosity. First, trust God, and then, let go of your banana!

"For where your treasure is, there your heart will be also."
Matthew 6:21 (New International Version)

#348 Inflation

Theme: Stewardship

Are you feeling pain?

This disease is called cirrhosis of the giver. The symptoms are pain in the financial area. It is often accompanied by paralysis or sudden loss of memory when exploring a generous lifestyle. There are side effects, including sporadic delusions—viewing money as larger than reality.

Do you support God's work with the same amount you gave five years ago? Expenses may be more today because of inflation. However, there is a greater issue: a biblical strategy.

Here's Our Prescription:

God's approach is to give a percentage. If you get a raise, does God's work get a raise? If you are blessed with inheritance, does God's work get a blessing? Think about it: If you are blessed, it is a gift from God. Make sure cirrhosis of the giver doesn't keep you from the joy of giving generously for God's work!

"'No one can serve two masters. Either you will hate the one and love the other, or you will be devoted to the one and despise the other. You cannot serve both God and money.'"
Matthew 6:24 (New International Version)

#349 Show Me the Money! Theme: Stewardship

Are you thankful?

Did you thank God for all the car accidents you didn't have this year? How about the illnesses you never developed? What about the home break-in that never occurred? Consider this: Americans sixty-five years old and older are worth, collectively, way more than $8.5 trillion. If one person chose to give away $8.5 trillion at a rate of one million dollars a day, it would take 23,287 years to dispose of it!

Think how many of us—at any age—are Christians. Consider how much God has given us. The Scripture says, "To whom much is given, much is required." It is not a law. It is an opportunity!

Here's Our Prescription:

You could help finance God's mission, here at home and around the world. In fact, if a number of Christians had not invested in Church Doctor Ministries, you would not be reading this! Ministry doesn't "just happen." God trusts you with finances. Think about how you could faithfully invest in God's eternal work. It is amazing how God works. You can make a difference in this world and simultaneously have an impact for the next!

"Now it is required that those who have been given a trust must prove faithful."
1 Corinthians 4:2 (New International Version)

#350 Faith Promise

Theme: Stewardship

Are you giving by faith?

The minister prayed, "Lord, protect us from members of this church who, when it comes to giving, stop at nothing." Some Christians give nothing back to God: no time, no use of their gifts, no portion of their money. At the other end of generosity, many respond to special opportunities with a faith promise. A faith promise is NOT dependent on your ability to pay. It is your willingness to be dependent on God to supply.

Our church asked everyone to give a special, extra financial gift for a new sound system. We said a faith promise prayer. "Lord, we want to give, so we are making an extravagant pledge by faith, trusting that You will supply our needs." That night, my parents called to say that they were sending us a financial gift.

Here's Our Prescription:

When you have a heart to give, but not the cash, make a promise, by faith. Trust God to supply, and when He does, give generously. Experience God's awesome power!

"And God, who supplies seed for the sower and bread to eat, will also supply you with all the seed you need and will make it grow and produce a rich harvest from your generosity."
2 *Corinthians 9:10 (Good News Translation)*

#351 The Light

Theme: Commitment

Are you sharing your faith?

The doctor was called to the rural home of a woman in labor. With no electricity, he asked the husband to hold a lantern. A baby was born, and the man began to lower the lantern. "No, keep it up. There's one more coming." The man lowered the lamp again, but the doctor said again, "Oops, there's another one—you have triplets!" The astonished father said, "Do you think the light is attracting them?"

Jesus is the light of the world. He attracts spiritually hungry people to be born again.

Here's Our Prescription:

Pray for opportunities to share your "God stories" with those who are far from God. You likely have dozens of stories about how God has worked in your life. By sharing your stories, you encourage others in times of joy and sorrow. Stories are powerful! Jesus is the Divine Storyteller. His stories are often called parables. Cultivate relationships and tell what God has done in your life. God will use your stories. The light of Christ shines through you—and attracts others to Jesus!

"You are like light for the whole world.... In the same way your light must shine before people, so that they will see the good things you do and praise your Father in heaven."

Matthew 5:14a, 16 (Good News Translation)

#352 Revival

Theme: Commitment

Want to grow spiritually?

You can call it a personal revival, spiritual renewal, or spiritual growth. With God's help, you turn from your sins and toward God. It is called "repentance." It is taking your eyes off yourself and focusing on God's agenda for your life.

Do you need a spiritual jump start? Would you like to impact this world for good? Do you want to change the spiritual atmosphere for yourself and others?

Here's Our Prescription:

Everyone wants to change the world, but few want to change themselves. Begin your day by praying, "Lord, bring revival, beginning with me." Read Scripture. Listen to God. Changing this world occurs one person at a time. Change your focus. Ask God to begin with you.

"Even though our physical being is gradually decaying, yet our spiritual being is renewed day after day."
2 Corinthians 4:16b (Good News Translation)

#353 Celebration

Theme: Commitment

Are you celebrating?

Celebrations are part of life. You celebrate birthdays, anniversaries, accomplishments, and holidays. You come together with friends and share joy and excitement. Worship is a time of celebration as well. You grow as God strengthens and encourages you. Richard Foster said, "Worship begins in holy expectancy; it ends in holy obedience.... To stand before the holy one of eternity is to change.... To worship is to change."

Here's Our Prescription:

Worship regularly. Prepare for worship with an attitude of openness. Expect God to show up and do something special in your life. Worship vertically as you connect with your Creator. Worship horizontally as you fellowship with friends. Let go; let God move in your life. Let God use worship to change you.

"Come, let us bow down and worship him; let us kneel before the Lord, our Maker! He is our God; we are the people he cares for, the flock for which he provides."

Psalm 95:6-7a (Good News Translation)

#354 Divine Conversation Theme: Commitment

Are you talking with God?

What do you know about prayer? I had a parrot. All it said was, "I want a kiss. I want a kiss." I took it to a friend's house. He had a parrot that said, "I want to pray. I want to pray." My parrot said, "I want a kiss." My friend's parrot responded, "My prayers are answered!" In truth? Prayer is actually a "conversation of love" between you and your Creator. It is a divine conversation. You share with God, and He shares with you.

Here's Our Prescription:

Think "thought" prayers as life occurs around you. You can pray through the Bible, verse by verse. Pray with thanksgiving, while trusting in God's promises. Develop a divine conversation. You will discover that God is more active in your life. And, you will become more active in His work.

"If we don't know how or what to pray, it doesn't matter. He does our praying in and for us, making prayer out of our wordless sighs, our aching groans. He knows us far better than we know ourselves, knows our pregnant condition, and keeps us present before God. That's why we can be so sure that every detail in our lives of love for God is worked into something good."
Romans 8:26b-28 (The Message)

#355 What's New?

Theme: Commitment

Do you make resolutions?

Have you ever made New Year's resolutions? I read that fifty-five percent of Americans keep their New Year's resolutions for less than one month. So, what would your resolution be? Lose weight? Spend more time with your family? Attend worship? Church is a great environment to help with your resolutions.

Here's Our Prescription:

Gather some Christian friends together into a "resolution fellowship." Meet together regularly. Encourage one another. Hold each other accountable. There is strength in numbers! Surrounded by Christian friends, you can help keep those resolutions. Pray for God's help. God's power helps you become a better you. Why wouldn't God help you become who He wants you to be? Make a resolution to ask for God's help.

"So let's walk right up to him and get what he is so ready to give. Take the mercy, accept the help."
Hebrews 4:16 (The Message)

#356 Retool

Theme: Commitment

Are you ready to change?

How many church members does it take to change a light bulb? Who said anything about change? When I started pastoring a small church in the country, Lloyd came up to me and said, "Pastor, I was here long before you came, and I'll be here after you leave. And in the meantime, I'm not changing." Well, Lloyd was right. He was there before I came, he was there after I left, and he didn't change!

Do you resist change? Would you like to change that?

Here's Our Prescription:

Keep yourself flexible. Be open to God. Jesus said, "I make all things new again." Christianity requires a commitment to change—for the better, to become more like God. Faith is a commitment to grow, with His help. There are two constant realities in this world: Jesus and change. Why not be eager for both?

> *"...anyone who belongs to Christ has become a new person. The old life is gone; a new life has begun!"*
> *2 Corinthians 5:17 (New Living Translation)*

#357 Focused Commitment

Theme: Commitment

Are you involved?

Dawson Trotman, founder of the Navigators, said, "Activity is no substitution for production. And production is no substitute for reproduction." If you are successful, when you die you might leave behind a house, a car, perhaps some land, a business, and some cash. But if you are eternally significant, you will have spiritually reproduced yourself. If you have been spiritually significant, you will have reproduced other believers.

Here's Our Prescription:

Commit to discipling others. Pour your Christian life into a few. Witness, share, encourage. Equip them for ministry. Follow six steps: (1) Come follow me; (2) I do/you watch; (3) I do/you help; (4) you do/I help; (5) you do/I watch; (6) we both go disciple another. Jesus did it with the disciples. The disciples did it with others. You will multiply for eternity.

"Go, then, to all peoples everywhere and make them my disciples: baptize them in the name of the Father, the Son, and the Holy Spirit, and teach them to obey everything I have commanded you. And I will be with you always, to the end of the age."
Matthew 28:19-20 (Good News Translation)

#358 Joy to the World   Theme: Joy

Where is your joy?

Have you ever said, "This will be the greatest Christmas ever"? I thought the first one was! From where do we get joy? Is it the presents, parties, or tinsel on the trees? The Christmas song is right: "Joy to the World," because "The Lord has come!"

Some think that real joy is when you don't have any difficulties. Joy is not the absence of trouble. It is the presence of Christ.

Here's Our Prescription:

To spread the joy, spread the good news about Jesus. Why? Because real joy occurs when people meet the Lord. Use the Christmas story to witness Jesus 24/7/365. After all, there is more joy in heaven over one sinner who repents than over ninety-nine who "don't need to."

"...Don't be afraid! I am here with good news for you, which will bring great joy to all the people. This very day in David's town your Savior was born – Christ the Lord!"
Luke 2:10-11 (Good News Translation)

#359 Who's Happy? Theme: Joy

Are you smiling?

"Hallelujah" means "hooray for God." It reflects that you are excited about Jesus in your life. There is a lot of joy in the world if you are a Christian. Jesus said, "Blessed are the peacemakers." "Blessed" means to be happy.

Yet, unfortunately, life is not always happy, even for believers. Sometimes, it seems like the only way to wake up in the morning with a smile on your face is to sleep with a coat hanger in your mouth.

Here's Our Prescription:

Turn to the Lord every day, asking for strength. He is the one who invites you to come to Him. Trust in Jesus, in good times—and difficult times. He is the true source of strength and joy. When you see others who are overwhelmed with challenges, share the Lord. Go way beyond happy. Find joy in Jesus.

"I have told you this so that my joy may be in you
and that your joy may be complete."
John 15:11 (Good News Translation)

#360 Christmas Joy! Theme: Joy

Do you ever wonder if God is for real?

Some second graders were talking about whether Santa Claus was real. One girl said she heard he wasn't, but she wasn't buying it. When asked why, she said, "Because my sister said Santa wasn't real. Right away, she stopped getting toys and started getting clothes."

The miracle of Christmas is that Jesus is real. He makes a difference in life. Joy is not a luxury. It is a sign that God is alive. Christmas joy is not a holiday fad but a year-round reality.

Here's Our Prescription:

Make a commitment to spread the joy of Jesus to everyone you meet. How? *Be* the joy, even when you face challenges. Demonstrate God's love in your words and actions. And don't be shy about it among those who are not *yet* believers. Live the miracle and joy of Christmas all year long!

"Rejoice in the Lord always. I will say it again: Rejoice!"
Philippians 4:4 (New International Version)

#361 Why Do You Sometimes Struggle? — Theme: Joy

Are you struggling?

If you are a Christian, it doesn't mean you have no challenges. Think of Jesus. He wasn't born in a palace, but a stable. A Sunday school teacher once asked the class, "What comes to mind when you think of Christmas?" Susie said, "I think of Mary, Joseph, baby Jesus, and Pontius the pilot." The teacher replied, "Pontius the pilot?" "Yeah," said Susie. "He was there for the flight into Egypt." When Jesus was born, people were out to kill Him. All His life, "religious" people were out to get Him.

Here's Our Prescription:

Don't be confused. The joy of Christmas isn't life without challenges. It IS life with God. Put life into perspective. Real joy isn't based on what happens to you, but on how you respond. The Bible says you can do all things through Christ who strengthens you! Believe that every day, and feel the joy.

"We pray that you'll have the strength to stick it out over the long haul – not the grim strength of gritting your teeth but the glory-strength God gives. It is strength that endures the unendurable and spills over into joy, thanking the Father who makes us strong enough to take part in everything bright and beautiful that he has for us."
Colossians 1:11-12 (The Message)

#362 Choose Joy   Theme: Joy

Do you wonder if Jesus ever laughed?

There have been many artistic paintings of Jesus created over the centuries. In many of them, He looks depressed, angry, or stern. Can you picture Jesus laughing, telling a good joke, or really enjoying Himself? I'm sure He did!

Here's Our Prescription:

If you want to share the good news about Jesus, and you want anybody to listen—it needs to sound like good news. I am not suggesting you "fake" it when you are sad. But if there is joy in your heart—tell your face. Too many believers look like they were baptized in vinegar! If you have joy in Christ—let it show in your attitude. If you are making "a joyful noise to the Lord"—smile! If you want to win others, be winsome. Don't ignore the challenges of life; just don't hide the joy.

"...may all who search for you be filled with joy and gladness in you. May those who love your salvation repeatedly shout, 'The LORD is great!'"
Psalm 40:16 (New Living Translation)

#363 Silly Putty

Theme: Joy

Who shapes your life?

When you were a kid, did you ever play with Silly Putty? You could mold and shape it to be just about anything. What shapes your life? The Bible says you are like clay. And God wants to shape you.

Many people in the world have a different set of values. Yet, if you are shaped by the world, you are manipulated like Silly Putty. Would you like to be shaped and molded by God Himself?

Here's Our Prescription:

Do what He wants. Read your Bible every day. Follow His truth. Hang out with other believers. Pray every day: "God, shape me! Show me Your will. Lead the way." Avoid anything that draws you away from God. Let the Lord mold you! You'll be in good shape for life and eternity.

"But you are our father, Lord. We are like clay, and you are like the potter. You created us…."
Isaiah 64:8 (Good News Translation)

#364 Happiness or Joy? Theme: Joy

Are you searching for happiness?

Have you learned the difference between happiness and joy? The word "happy" is used in the Bible to describe a temporary, positive feeling. It is found only thirty-two times in Scripture. A variety of experiences can bring happiness, but the word "joy" describes the permanent feeling of *hope in God*. Only God can provide it. Even during difficult times, it is possible to experience joy in the Lord. "Joy" is in the Bible 236 times!

Unlike happiness, nothing can steal your joy. Are you a joyful person?

Here's Our Prescription:

Face adversity with the joy of the Lord. It means, with God's help, you have *hope* on an eternal scale. The presence of Jesus puts challenges into proper perspective. Happiness? It is here today and gone tomorrow. Joy lasts forever. This is what it means to say, "Hope springs eternal." God's hope for you, in you, lasts forever. Who wouldn't want that joy?

"Count it all joy, my brethren, when you meet various trials…."
James 1:2 (Revised Standard Version)

#365 Scared about the Future? Theme: Joy

Are you afraid?

Fear is your enemy. He wants to rob your energy, your joy, your confidence, and your progress. Older translations of the Bible say you should "fear" God. What is that about? Today, that word would be translated "respect." Yet, we Christians do experience fear of failure, especially when God stretches us. It often occurs when He challenges us to do something new or different.

In your faith life, do you ever find yourself backing away because you are afraid?

Here's Our Prescription:

Look in the mirror. Define your value by the God who made you—not by what you do. Failure is an event that occurs. It is never who you are. Jesus was beaten, nailed to a cross, and killed. Was He a failure? No! It was His love at work. Why? So you will never be a failure in God's eyes. Let God stretch you. His love drives away all fear. That is never failure. It is divine success!

"Don't panic. I'm with you. There's no need to fear
for I'm your God. I'll give you strength. I'll help you.
I'll hold you steady, keep a firm grip on you."
Isaiah 41:10 (The Message)

Acknowledgments

This unique daily devotional was birthed by a vision generated in Petoskey, Michigan. Jim, Ben, Mark, Tom, and Dan are some of the most creative and committed Christians I have ever met. They pitched the idea of "The Church Doctor" on Christian radio. Through the vehicle of Ambassador Advertising Agency in California, the short vignettes were aired on Christian radio, Monday through Friday, on 250 Christian radio stations in the US, England, Canada, and worldwide—broadcast out of Quito, Ecuador.

After several years of broadcasting, the board for Church Doctor Ministries chose to repurpose the radio platform to that of a daily devotional. The demand for engaging content for radio was redirected to the written page in a process that required numerous edits. Since the content format was originally geared to radio listeners, there is a "punch line" at the end of each daily "dose of Scripture." I am grateful to our friends at Ambassador Advertising for raising the bar of discipline so high.

I thank God for our amazing team at Church Doctor Ministries: Matt, Chelsey, Aaron, Jason, Katie, John, Tom, Todd, Chrysanne, Beth, Becca, and Carol. Our leader, Tracee Swank, provides outstanding guidance for our entire team. I thank God for the amazing gifts God has given Tracee and the way He blesses our work to help Christians and churches become more impactful to reach their communities for Jesus Christ.

I thank God for my wife, Janet, who works by my side in the final edits. She always makes the final product so much better!

Jason Atkinson, who serves as my assistant, is the most dedicated servant I have ever known. His efforts influence every page.

Finally, I want to thank the members of the two churches we attend: St. Mark's and Classic City—the same church in two locations, each with a different style of worship. Several people from these churches have used early copies of *An Apple a Day*. Your excitement and enthusiasm about your experience has been a great encouragement. Thank you, Pastor Jon, for your outstanding leadership!

About the Authors

Kent R. Hunter is the founder of Church Doctor Ministries. He has served as a pastor in Michigan, Indiana, and South Australia. In the past 38 years, Kent has consulted more than 1,800 churches from 78 denominations, fellowships, and movements. (Kent was trained by Lyle Schaller. Schaller edited one of Kent's books, *Your Church Has Personality: Find Your Focus, Maximize Your Mission*, published by Abingdon Press.) Kent is the architect of the SEND Movement (a 36-month mission training movement for individual churches) and SEND (a training experience to equip young adults and adults of any age to be missionaries to their own culture). Kent is a retired, ordained pastor in the Lutheran Church—Missouri Synod. Each year, he consults churches, interviewing hundreds of people in one-on-one interviews. He is invited to speak before numerous groups. Kent is a personal guide/coach for several leaders.

Kent received his Master of Divinity degree from Concordia Seminary, St. Louis, Missouri, and a Ph.D. from Lutheran School of Theology at Chicago. He earned the Doctor of Ministry degree at Fuller Theological Seminary, Pasadena, California, where he learned mission strategy. He is the author of several books on the subject of church health, vitality, and the effectiveness of the Christian movement.

Tracee J. Swank serves as the leader of Church Doctor Ministries and is a certified Church Doctor consultant, a Christian leadership coach, a certified Building a StoryBrand/Marketing Made Simple Guide, and a licensed Business Made Simple Entrepreneur Coach. Tracee is passionate about resourcing and releasing Christian leaders to help fulfill the Great Commission through coaching, consulting, and teaching. She leads the ministry staff team, trains and develops Church Doctor coaches and consultants, and oversees the advancement of the mission for the ministry.

Tracee has a Bachelor of Arts degree from the University of Toledo. She received a Master of Arts (Theological Studies with a concentration in Christian Spirituality) from Winebrenner Theological Seminary. Tracee is currently pursuing a Doctor of Ministry degree researching the role spiritual entrepreneurship plays in the growth of churches, outreach ministries, and marketplace mission-focused businesses.

Made in USA - Crawfordsville, IN
77305_9798843441050
12.05.2022 1235